MY GOD IS REAL

Sir:
You recently sent me 1 copy of ——
by —— Watson. I was reading it with pleasure the
other morning when I suddenly realized an interruption —
pp. 32–48 are missing.
I suspect in such cases you make it good by a
replacement. If you wish ~~the~~ my copy back — I shall
return it after receiving the new one — so I can
transfer the markings.
Thank you.

My God is real

DAVID C K WATSON

THE SEABURY PRESS • NEW YORK

First *Seabury Paperback* edition 1970

Library of Congress Catalog Card Number: 70-122630
691-970-C-5
Printed in the United States of America

Contents

To Anne

Introducing David Watson

David Watson, or David C. K. Watson to be exact (there being another well-known evangelical by the name of David Watson), has probably spoken face to face with as many, if not more, British students over the past few years as any other Christian preacher. The chapters in this book are based on addresses he has delivered to undergraduates at Cambridge University and elsewhere.

Born in 1933, he himself was converted as an undergraduate at Cambridge and later was ordained into the ministry of the Church of England. After curacies at Gillingham and Cambridge, he went in 1965 to a city centre church in York that was on the redundant list. Within the first week at York, members of the redundancy commission called saying 'What are we going to do with you after we close St Cuthbert's?'

In 1968 students of York University conducted a campaign protesting at the money wasted maintaining many of York's unsupported church buildings. As part of that campaign they placed pickets at the door of St Cuthbert's to check how many people attended the morning service. With about five minutes to go before the service started, David came out to meet them with a twinkle in his small, hooded eyes, inviting them to join the congregation before there were no more places left! Today it is not unknown for people to have to be turned away from an overfull church.

What is David's secret? He is certainly not a strikingly handsome, magnetic personality. Rather he is a typical product of the British public school ethos, of medium height, pleasant but not distinctive voice and unremarkable dress sense. He is not an intellectual and he makes no attempt to be 'way out'–in fact he is disgustingly 'square' and almost 'establishment'! When he speaks–and 'speaking' rather than 'preaching' is the operative word–there are three qualities that stand out a mile and are curiously compelling. First, it is clear that he genuinely believes and is utterly committed to all that he says. Secondly, no one could ever accuse him of putting on an act. There is a naturalness and honesty that is refreshing and relaxing. Thirdly, while he makes no attempt to be an intellectual, what he says comes over as immensely reasonable. I have seen students who came to the meetings expecting a crusading zealot lose their scepticism and sit back thoughtfully as they realized they were not going to be 'got at'.

He is very difficult to dislike. While no humourist, and certainly not a 'gag cracker', he nevertheless bubbles over with a quiet humour and sense of enjoyment in all that he does. He respects his audiences and evokes their respect in return. But when one has seen the numbers who have responded to his low-key unadorned biblical preaching, one is left convinced that the real secret must be that the God he talks about is real and uses him.

Gavin Reid

Introduction

A desire for reality is almost universal. If at the moment there is a revolt against the established Christian Church, it is in part a healthy distaste for all that is hollow and humbug. 'Somehow God has become for most people, and even for many practising Christians, unreal', writes Bernadine Bishop. 'The God we want must be real. He must be a convincing personal experience. The God who is not real to me, revealing and operating all that is deepest and most personal in my being, is no God to me.'[1] Fair enough! The question is: how can God become real, if indeed He exists at all?

This is a question which many have asked. 'My soul thirsts for God, for the living God', cried the psalmist.[2] 'Oh, that I knew where I might find him', complained Job.[3] 'I sought him, but found him not; I called him, but he gave no answer', recounts the bride in the Song of Solomon.[4] Michel Quoist expresses the feelings of many:

> *Lord, do you hear me?...*
> *Lord, I can no longer find my own door.*
> *I grope around blindly,*
> *I knock against my own walls, my own boundaries.*
> *I hurt myself,*
> *I am in pain...*
> *Lord, Lord, do you hear me?*
> *Lord, show me my door,*
> *take me by the hand.*
> *Open the door,*
> *Show me the way,*
> *The path leading to* joy, *to* light.
> *But, Lord, do you hear me?*[5]

Why is this search for the reality of God so important?

[1] Bernadine Bishop: *The God I want* p 141
[2] 42.2 [3] 23.3 [4] 3.1
[5] Michel Quoist: *Prayers of Life* (Logos Books), pp 87–88

First, there is today a general restlessness. If there is disillusionment concerning conventional established Christianity, there is also dissatisfaction with what is apparently the only alternative. Colin Wilson, a confessed rebel against the Establishment, states that he is still searching for a 'perfect freedom': 'We need a new religion to unite us and give us purpose...my deepest interest is religion. My deepest need–to create my own.' In other words he, together with the great majority, is searching for reality. We see this restlessness expressed in pop songs and modern films, whether by the Beatles or Bergman.

According to Pascal there is a conflict between reason and the passions. If only man had 'reason without passions...if he had only passions without reason...but having both, he cannot be without strife, being unable to be at peace with the one without being at war with the other'.[1] The conflict is revealed in sexual licence, experiments with drugs, and the persistent search for an 'ultimate' experience. All this is simply an attempt to discover the true meaning of life.

Secondly, in the minds of a great many people, there is a distorted image of the Christian faith. When my father died I was going through some family papers and possessions, and I came across an old painting of one of my ancestors. It looked rather dusty, and in my impatience I wanted to throw it into the dustbin, where it seemed to belong. As far as I was concerned it was a useless relic of bygone days. Many have the same impatience with Christianity: 'a useless relic of bygone days'. However, I did not throw the picture into the dustbin, and today I am very glad. It was found to be an extremely valuable painting, and suddenly this dreary dusty ancestral portrait acquired a new respect from the members of our family! And I would suggest that if, at the moment, many are tempted to reject the Christian faith as a useless relic, they may be in for a great surprise.

Christ Himself said that the Christian life could be thought of as treasure discovered in a field, or a pearl of great price. Therefore the heart of the Christian faith is something precious and of great value. The person who thinks that Christ wants to turn his life into a musty old attic filled with

[1] Pascal: *Penseés* No. 412

outdated ideas has not begun to understand the true meaning of being a Christian. Christ said: 'I have come that men may have life, and may have it in all its fullness' (John 10.10 NEB).

Thirdly, Christ said some startling things about Himself and our relationship with Him. We shall be looking at some of these more fully in the rest of this book; but in the Sermon on the Mount He said:

> 'Not everyone who calls me "Lord, Lord" will enter the kingdom of Heaven, but only those who do the will of my heavenly Father. When that day comes, many will say to me, "Lord, Lord, did we not prophesy in your name, cast out devils in your name, and in your name perform many miracles?" Then I will tell them to their face, "I never knew you: out of my sight, you and your wicked ways!"' (Matthew 7.21–3 NEB)

According to Jesus Christ, we shall all one day have to give an account of our lives; and on that day, the Day of Judgment, the crucial question will be 'What place has Christ had in your life?'

If the things Christ said are not true, then the sooner we throw this Christianity into a funeral pyre the better. Many down the centuries, have tried to do so, and many would like to do it today. If Christ's words are not true, our churches can become bingo halls, the Bible can go into a museum, ministers and missionaries can stop wasting their time; and thousands of Christians throughout the world can stop being persecuted for the sake of their Master.

On the other hand, if Christ's teaching is the truth, the position is very different. There may need to be radical changes in our lives, a new life altogether. What is necessary is that we should know what real Christianity is all about: and that is the purpose of this book.

One final point of introduction. God never promises to reveal Himself purely to satisfy our intellectual curiosity. There is one essential condition, and that is honesty. The person who is determined to justify his unbelief will never discover that God is real. But to the one who is honest in his search, honest about his doubts and confusion, honest about his intellectual problems, and honest enough to examine the evidence with as fresh and open a mind as he can bring to it, God will make Himself known.

I found this to be true in my own experience when I went up to university as a professing humanist. I had never found the reality of God in my own life, and therefore tried to convince myself that He simply did not exist. However, with the help of a friend, I looked at the Christian faith again, acted on the evidence I could see, and since that time have not doubted that MY GOD IS REAL.

CHAPTER ONE

The Man who is God

We must start at the right place; and the right place in our search for the reality of God is the person of Jesus Christ. Dr Griffith Thomas once wrote: 'Christianity is the only religion in the world which rests on the person of its founder'.[1]

Some may think that this is the wrong starting-point. They would say that it is pointless to try to prove that Christ is the *Son* of God when they cannot believe in God's existence in the first place. 'Prove God's existence first,' they would say, 'then we will consider our attitude to Christ.'

However, our reason for starting at Christ is important. What do men know about God, from their own natural wisdom? Virtually nothing. As soon as man begins to seek for God he is baffled and confused, groping in the dark, out of his depth. Nor should it surprise us that he feels lost in his search for God, because if God exists He is infinite, and man is finite. How could a finite being possibly comprehend Infinity? Paul said that man by wisdom cannot know God and cannot find God; God is altogether beyond his reach. We should all be incurably agnostic if God had not revealed Himself. But the Christian contention is that God has revealed Himself: through the Old Testament prophets, through the Jewish nation, through the Scriptures, but supremely in the person of Jesus Christ; and Christ is therefore rightly our starting-point.

Most people would agree that Christ was at least a good religious teacher. I have never yet met anyone who has seriously questioned this, though many would add that He was nothing more. All too often people are quick to dismiss the Christian faith because of some inconsistency they can see in the professing Christian world round them, but very seldom are such critics thorough in their examination of the person of Christ Himself.

[1] G. Thomas: *Christianity is Christ* (Longmans, 1925), p 7.

Who is Jesus Christ? This question is often asked in the Gospels. On one occasion He calmed a storm on the Sea of Galilee, and His disciples asked: 'What sort of man is this?' (Matthew 8.27). On another, He made some devastating claims about Himself, and His opponents asked, 'Who on earth do you think you are?' Christ Himself asked, 'Who do men say that I am?' (Mark 8.27).

The disciples were convinced of the divinity of Christ, not by theological argument, but by personal experience over the greater part of three years. We know, said John, because 'we have heard,...we have seen with our eyes...and touched with our hands' (1 John 1.1). What evidence brought them to this unshakable conclusion?

His Claims

We are not limited to stories of His power as it was demonstrated two thousand years ago. He is still revealing Himself in astonishing ways in the lives of people today; but for the moment I want to concentrate primarily on the New Testament.

(1) *Indirect Claims. His miracles.* The evidence for His divinity does not rest on these, but they were so striking that great crowds gathered round Him. When a paralysed man was brought to Him, He immediately said, with authority, 'Your sins are forgiven'. The Scribes (the bright theologians of the time) who were present, knew perfectly well what this implied. Their cry was: 'It is blasphemy! Who can forgive sins but God alone?' And Christ, intending to drive home this very conclusion, replied 'That you may know that the Son of Man has authority on earth to forgive sins' (and then he turned to the paralysed man) 'I say to you, rise, take up your pallet and go home'. And immediately the man got up, took up his bed, and walked off. And they were all astounded.[1]

Take another example. Thomas, the disciple, was filled with doubts about the divinity and resurrection of Christ. So the risen Christ came to him and said 'Put your finger here, and see my hands; and put out your hand, and place it in my side'.[2] In other words, 'Touch my scars, see for yourself!' Thomas answered, 'My Lord and my God'. Now what did

[1] Mark 2.1–12 [2] John 20.26–9

Christ do? Did He say 'Thomas, you must never call Me that. I am not your God'? Not at all. He accepted the worship of this disciple. He allowed him to call Him 'My God'. Indeed, He gently rebuked him for his unbelief, because he had never trusted in Christ's divinity before. If we read on to the Acts of the Apostles, and see Paul and Barnabas healing a cripple at Lystra, we find a striking contrast. When the miracle occurred the crowds came out of the temple with oxen and garlands to offer sacrifices to Paul and Barnabas, because they believed that they must surely be gods. Paul and Barnabas were horrified. 'Why are you doing this? We also are men, of like nature with you, and bring you good news, that you should turn from these vain things to a living God.'[1] Yet Christ calmly accepted as His right the worship of His disciple.

His teaching

Two things are clear about Christ's teaching. First, it is incredibly self-centred; secondly, if it is true, it is of enormous importance for us today. People are hungry and thirsty for something which satisfies; they know deep within themselves that their lives are empty. Jesus said, 'I am the bread of life... if anyone eats of this bread, he will live for ever'.[2] I am the Living Water; 'if anyone thirst, let him come to me and drink'.[3] Many today are searching for God, but they do not know where to find Him, or even whether He exists. Jesus said, 'I am the way, and the truth, and the life; no one comes to the Father, but by me'.[4] Many are stumbling through this life, groping in the dark, with little or no direction and purpose. Jesus said, 'I am the light of the world; he who follows me will not walk in darkness, but will have the light of life.[5] Many are living under stress and conscious of the terrifying pressures of our modern world. Jesus said, 'Come to me, all who labour and are heavy laden, and I will give you rest'.[6] Many feel that they can do nothing of ultimate value. Jesus said, 'I am the vine, you are the branches. He who abides in me...bears much fruit'.[7] All of us, one day, must

[1] Acts 14.8–18 [2] John 6.35, 51 [3] John 7.37
[4] John 14.6 [5] John 6.48–51; 7.37; 14.6; 8.12
[6] Matthew 11.28 [7] John 15.5

face death and life after death. Jesus said, 'I am the resurrection and the life; he who believes in me...shall never die'.[1] 'I am the good shepherd...and I give...eternal life'. 'I am the door; if anyone enters by me, he will be saved.'[2]

So we could multiply examples. And yet some say that He was no more than a good religious teacher!

Direct Claims

In John 10.30 Christ said, 'I and the Father are one', meaning 'one in substance'. And it is perfectly clear that the Jews knew how to interpret this because in the next verse we read 'they took up stones...again to stone him'. Stoning was the penalty for blasphemy and if Christ's words were not true then he was clearly an outrageous blasphemer.

In John 14.9 Christ said, 'He who has seen me has seen the Father'. The context of this is important. Philip, together with the other disciples, had various doubts about the person of Christ. 'Lord, show us the Father, and we shall be satisfied.' In others words, he was asking to see the reality of God before he could fully trust himself to Jesus Christ. This was not just an academic question: Philip and the others were in earnest, they meant business. They realized that, if they were to follow Christ at all, theirs must be nothing less than a wholehearted discipleship, whatever the cost might be. Christ had just told them that there would come a time when they would be tested and persecuted; that one of their number would betray Him: and that He Himself would be crucified. He went on to tell them not to worry about these things, and spoke to them of the certainty of heaven. Wonderfully comforting words! But the disciples' reaction is understandable and indeed, contemporary: 'Unless I can be quite sure, why on earth should I commit myself to this way of life, let alone to a person, to one who is going to be martyred, to one who tells me that I, too, may be martyred, and that anyway I must put him first! That is quite a lot to stomach! I don't mind coming to church occasionally, saying my prayers, helping my neighbour. But I'm not at all sure about getting really involved with Christ, whatever the cost might be.'

[1] John 11.25–26 John 11.25–6; 10.14, 27–8,9

I think that something like this was going on in the mind of Philip when he said, 'Show us the Father and we shall be satisfied'. It was a fair question, and it is a fair question today. In some parts of the world it is not at all easy for the man or woman who becomes a Christian:

> 'I myself was later in prison, together with souls whom God had helped me to win for Christ. I was in the same cell with one who had left behind six children and who was now in prison for his Christian faith. His wife and children were starving. He might never see them again. I asked him: "Have you any resentment against me that I brought you to Christ and because of this your family is in such misery?" He said: "I have no words to express my thankfulness that you have brought me to the wonderful Saviour. I would never have it another way." '[1]

Of course, we may not face such a situation at the moment. Nevertheless, an active, committed Christian, unashamed of Christ, speaking to others about Him, is today very much out on a limb. As one young writer has expressed it:

> 'England has been officially Christian for more than fifteen hundred years. Our whole culture is based on Christianity. However, today it is apparently no longer respectable, or even acceptable, actually to *be* a Christian. This is especially so among people of my own age and type.
>
> 'Humanism is the thing. It is not that religion in general is out. Roman Catholics are just all right because one is generally born a Catholic and so cannot do anything about it. Mormons are O.K. too, not to *be*, but for sociological study purposes. The Eastern religions are very trendy. But as for ordinary God-fearing, Bible-reading, Christ-imitating Christianity – it's plain old-fashioned. You're barmy, a freak, if you believe it in these days.'[2]

That is a widespread viewpoint. Today, people are very interested to hear about the Christian faith, but very unwilling to commit themselves personally. Why? Because today it is not easy to be a true disciple of Jesus Christ. You are a marked man, or woman. It costs something.

That is why Philip's question is so relevant: 'Show us the Father and we shall be satisfied.' We want to be sure. And

[1] R. Wurmbrand: *Tortured for Christ* (Hodder and Stoughton, 1967), p 27 f

[2] *Weekend Telegraph*

Christ replied, 'He who has seen me has seen the Father'. That is a wonderful statement! At last we can know something about God, because here is a man who *is* God!

Perhaps the most important of all His direct claims comes in John chapter 8, where Jesus is in controversy with the Jews. 'Your father Abraham rejoiced that he was to see my day; he saw it and was glad,' said Jesus. 'You are not yet fifty years old', and yet they protested, 'have you seen Abraham?'

Christ replied, 'Truly, truly, I say to you, before Abraham was, I am'. And immediately the Jews took up stones to stone Him to death. That '*I AM*' was God's own name, revealed to Moses[1] yet Jesus calmly took this divine title for Himself. Nothing could have been clearer. In the words of the late William Temple: 'It is now recognized that the one Christ for whose existence there is any evidence at all is a miraculous figure making stupendous claims.'

And yet some say that He was no more than a good religious teacher.

His Character

His claims were supported at every point by His character. As Tennyson said, 'His character was more wonderful than the greatest miracle'. We could spend a long time looking at His poise, His majesty, His love, His humility, His thoughtfulness, His devotion. Wherever He went He cared for the lonely, the sick, the social outcasts, and all in need. No one can fail to admire the beauty of His character; but there is one feature which makes Him unique, and that is His sinlessness. This is so remarkable that we should ask a number of witnesses for their evidence.

Let us ask His close friends. They were with Him constantly for nearly three years, and saw Him tired, tested and besieged by the crowds to the point of distraction. Yet Peter said that He was 'without blemish or spot'; 'He committed no sin; no guile was found on his lips'.[2] John said, 'If we say we have no sin, we deceive ourselves...' but of Jesus He said, 'In Him there is no sin'.[3] This is the testimony of two of His closest friends, and such close friends usually know the truth about us!

[1] Exodus 3,13–15
[2] 1 Peter 1.19; 2.22
[3] 1 John 1.8; 2.5

Let us ask His enemies. Of course, some of them engaged in a good deal of political mud-slinging. Some called Him a Sabbath-breaker, a 'wine-bibber', a subversive element, the friend of those whom society had rejected. Yet what happened when they were called upon seriously to examine His character? On one occasion Christ asked His critics, 'Which of you convicts me of sin?'[1] No one could answer. Pilate said, after careful examination, 'I did not find this man guilty of any of your charges against Him'.[2]

Let us then ask Christ Himself. He, indeed, would be guilty of sublime arrogance had anyone been able to show that His claims were false, but no one could. 'I always do what is pleasing to him.'[3] He was continually telling others to repent, yet He never repented Himself. He was always accusing the Pharisees of hearts that were dirty and full of sin, and yet Christ Himself had 'a conscience unclouded by the memory of any sin'.[4] Think how quickly these fantastic claims would have been challenged if they had not been genuine.

This at once puts Him in a class utterly distinct, not only from sinners, but also from saints. It is the universal experience of all godly men that the nearer they come to God, the more aware they are of sin.

> *'And they who fain would serve Thee best*
> *Are conscious most of wrong within.'*[5]

Not so Jesus Christ. As C. S. Lewis put it: 'The discrepancy between the depth, sincerity, and may I say, the shrewdness of His moral teaching, and the rampant megalomania which must lie behind His theological teaching unless He is God, has never been got over.' And yet some say that He was no more than a good religious teacher.

It should be fairly obvious by now that this is the one way in which we cannot describe Jesus Christ. No one in the Gospels ever thought that He was just a great man or a marvellous teacher, because this was an impossible conclusion. To be accurate, there was one person who tried to say this—the rich young ruler. 'Good Teacher,' he said, 'what must I

[1] John 8.46 [2] Luke 23.14 [3] John 8.29
[4] David Swanes, quoted in *Christianity is Christ*, p 18
[5] H. Twells

do to inherit eternal life?' And at once Christ came back at him: 'Why do you call me good? No one is good but God alone.'[1] In other words, 'good teacher' is an impossible description. He was saying: 'Either I am just a teacher, and in that case I am not good in God's eyes; I am a sinner like everyone else. Or, I am good, because I am God.' Therefore Christ was either very much more than a 'good teacher' or very much less. He cannot be damned with faint praise! He can be called evil, deluded, devil-possessed, a madman, a blasphemer. Some called Him precisely these things in His own day. But such judgments as these, when set against His character and teaching, tell us less about Christ than about the people who made them. To them Jesus said, 'By your words you will be condemned'.[2]

Who then is Jesus Christ? We have to be careful how we answer this because it is a boomerang question; it is not primarily an academic matter. Some people think that they can sit down and discuss the Christian faith as they might discuss a scientific hypothesis. This is not so. God does not prove His existence by a series of propostions; He reveals Himself in a Person, and the way in which we respond to a living person is very different, and much more demanding, than our response to a logical proposition. 'Christ's teaching therefore cannot be grasped by the intellect alone', wrote C. S. Lewis, 'cannot be "got up" as if it were a subject...He will not be, in the way we want, "pinned down". The attempt is (again I mean no irreverence), like trying to bottle a sunbeam.'

Primarily this is a moral issue, a challenge to the will. Paul said that judgment would come upon 'those who do not know God and who do not obey the gospel of our Lord Jesus'.[3] Therefore, the question is ultimately not one of understanding, but one of obeying. A Christian is called a 'disciple': one who follows Jesus, listens to Him and obeys Him.

People commonly ask the wrong questions about the Christian faith. Is it helpful? Is it satisfying? Is it worth my while? These are relatively unimportant. The vital issue is: *Is it true?* And Christ replies, 'I am...the Truth...no one comes to the Father, but by Me'.[4] Therefore, one who wants

[1] Mark 10.17–18 [2] Matthew 12.37
[3] 2 Thessalonians 1.8 [4] John 14.6

to know about God and find Him as a real person in his life, must come to Jesus. He alone can bring him into a living relationship with God Himself.

People often say to me, 'But it requires tremendous faith to believe all that! You cannot prove it conclusively. It goes far beyond logic and reason. Perhaps you are wrong.' One cannot in fact prove, logically, any person's existence, even one's own; it is a matter of experience. The Christian belief is therefore a step of faith, and it cannot be proved mathematically or scientifically. But it needs far greater faith to believe that Christianity is not true; that the historical facts of the Christian faith are fairy tales, that Christ's teaching is false; and that the experience of Christians all down the centuries has been based on a delusion.

There is a mass of evidence for what the Christian believes. But where is the evidence for the agnostic position? He has to believe, with the authority only of his personal opinion, that all that Christ taught was either not true or not important. Christ, with His life and actions supporting all that He said, stressed repeatedly that His teaching was authoritative and urgent. Any man who tries to think honestly must ask himself what it was that made Christ speak with such authority and why His message is so relevant for the modern world.

CHAPTER TWO

Sin—A Christian Neurosis?

We shall see something of the relevance of Christ if we look at the story of one likeable rebel, the young woman of Samaria, whose meeting with Christ is recorded in John 4.

Like many of her generation she was disillusioned because she saw that the established traditional life of her country had nothing to offer her that was real and satisfying. Socially, the Jews were not on speaking terms with the Samaritans. Social and racial distinctions were deep rooted. Politically, the country, under the Roman government, was 'going to the dogs'. Economically, times were hard; and here she was, poor thing, having to collect water every day from the only tap in the neighbourhood! Morally, there was a hypocritical veneer of respectability! The very people who complained about the morality of her generation were by no means innocent themselves, and sometimes a really juicy bit of aristocratic scandal would hit the headlines. Spiritually, of course, the country was dead. Theologians spent their time arguing whether God ought to be worshipped in Samaria or in Jerusalem. They were hopelessly out of touch with real life, and their teaching was completely irrelevant. I think she would have enjoyed William Temple's definition of a theologian as 'a man who spends his time answering questions that nobody is asking.' In particular, she could not stand the religious preoccupation with sin, always so guilt-ridden and introspective. 'Positively a neurosis,' she might have said. 'What's the point of being morbid all the time? Life's bleak enough as it is!'

The answer? Well, of course, to throw religion overboard. She was no fool. She was determined to get some kick out of life in a set-up which was otherwise extremely dreary. Unless she found some excitement, life was scarcely worth living. Therefore she let go some of her inhibitions, experimented with free love, and drew a large circle of friends. Three words more or less summed up her total ambition: *happiness*, *freedom, life.* That, perhaps, is a fair description of what most people are looking for today.

Disillusioned

However, she met with a number of surprises. In the first place, *her pursuit of happiness left her curiously unhappy and dissatisfied.* Playing around with men merely convinced her that most men were selfish creatures, out to satisfy their own lusts but knowing very little about love. Further, her search for happiness proved to be increasingly frustrating. Free love soon lost its initial thrill, and left a great deal of pain and sorrow behind it. The wide circle of 'friends' proved to be unreliable and selfish; she was still horribly lonely at times; she had no one to whom she could turn. Nor could she finally throw overboard all notions of God. There were various questions which still required an answer; and there was something else, a conscience, which nagged–maybe not very often, but every now and then, when she was in one of her more reflective moods. She had very little peace in her heart, although you might not have guessed it on casual acquaintance. In short, she was not particularly happy.

Of course, she was beginning to discover, the hard way, the truth about human nature. William Golding is one of today's writers who, in his book *The Lord of the Flies*, reminds us what human nature is really like. For too long we 'have never looked further than the rash appearing on the skin'; it is time we began to look 'for the root of the disease instead of describing the symptoms'. Therefore in his writings he lifts the lid and peers inside. He is not concerned with the externals: what man would like to be and what he tries to be in front of other people. He is concerned, as God is, with what man is like in his innermost being, in the secret of his heart. And he shows us, undeniably, that beneath the surface of our much-prized rationality there is a 'seething cauldron of untamed desire'. Yet, when we see this extremely unattractive picture, it is extraordinary how we try to talk ourselves out of it. We talk about inhibitions, complexes, twists in our nature, mistakes, and temperament. We do not like using the word which the Bible uses, and which Christ frequently used: sin.

Sometimes I hear the protest: 'I don't understand this concept of sin. I don't know what you mean.' However, it is also my experience that no one has any real problem about this concept. Everyone knows what it is to be selfish, to lie, hate, steal, cheat, lust, criticize and judge other people. Paul wrote:

'You therefore have no defence—you who sit in judgment, whoever you may be—for in judging your fellow-man you condemn yourself, since you, the judge, are equally guilty. It is admitted that God's judgment is rightly passed upon all who commit such crimes as these; and do you imagine—you who pass judgment on the guilty while committing the same crimes yourself—do you imagine that you, any more than they, will escape the judgment of God?' (Romans 2.1–3 NEB)

This is a common fault today—blaming someone else. 'It's them!' 'It's him!' 'It's her!' But it's never 'me'! C. S. Lewis, in his book *The Great Divorce*, talks about a meeting with a 'tousle-headed poet':

'He appeared to be a singularly ill-used man. His parents had never appreciated him and none of the five schools at which he had been educated seemed to have made any provision for a talent and temperament such as his. To make matters worse he had been exactly the sort of boy in whose case the examination system works out with the maximum unfairness and absurdity. It was not until he reached the university that he began to recognise that all these injustices did not come by chance but were the inevitable results of our economic system. Capitalism did not merely enslave the workers, it also vitiated taste and vulgarised intellect: hence our educational system and hence a lack of "Recognition" for new genius. This discovery had made him a Communist... There were money troubles. His father, who had never progressed beyond the most atrocious mental complacency and smugness of the Victorian epoch, was giving him a ludicrously inadequate allowance. And he had been very badly treated by a girl too. He had thought her a really civilised and adult personality, and then she had unexpectedly revealed that she was a mass of bourgeois prejudices and monogamic instincts. Jealousy, possessiveness, was a quality he particularly disliked. She had even shown herself, at the end, to be mean about money. That was the last straw...'[1]

[1] C. S. Lewis: *The Great Divorce* (Geoffrey Bles, 1946), p 17 f

It's him! It's her! It's them! *But it's never me!*

That is why the word 'sin' is so unpopular. It is too personal. Once I accept the concept of sin, I have to face up to the fact that I am responsible for my actions. I am guilty, and I need to be forgiven.

Christ taught a good deal about sin. He saw it as man's number one need for God. He saw it as corrupting and spoiling the life of every person born into the world. That is why He came: to 'save His people from their sins'.[1] He knew that unless the diagnosis of man was known and accepted, and unless the surgeon's knife could do its work, this cancer of sin would spread and kill.

Yet is it not incredible that some people are still optimistic about the quality of human nature? If we look back over history, every civilization has boasted of the achievements and abilities of man. We read of the Age of Enlightenment, the Age of Reason, the Golden Age. In the words of Professor James Stewart, 'The renaissance humanists thought that man was the measure of all things. His will was the architect of destiny. His intelligence, storming the secrets of the universe, had occupied the throne of God. "Thou art smitten, thou God", shouted Swinburne vociferously.

> "*Thou art smitten; thy death is upon thee, O Lord.*
> *And the love song of earth, as thou diest, resounds through the wind of her wings—*
> *Glory to man in the highest! for man is the master of things.*"[2]

Is man really the master of things? Look at Vietnam, Rhodesia, South Africa, China, race riots...and yet today we find the same silly optimism. Humanists say that man is well able to cope with himself and with the problems of the world, provided that he is not shackled by the immature creeds of religion. It is worth pointing out that humanism flourishes *only* in intellectual circles, where it is *easy* to be idealistic about life. As a minister, I am constantly faced with complex human and domestic problems; and in this ordinary world, of needy men and women, although many strange beliefs

[1] Matthew 1.21
[2] quoted in J. S. Stewart: *Teach Yourself Preaching*, p 14

exist, I scarcely ever encounter a convinced humanist. Once you step out of an intellectual greenhouse into the fierce storms of everyday life, you are forced to be realistic about human nature. You cannot be blind to the sin which exists in the heart of man. Dr C. E. M. Joad, who for many years embraced a 'rational-optimist philosophy', found his idealistic beliefs shattered in the last world war. He came to see that:

> 'evil is endemic in man, and that the Christian doctrine of original sin expresses a deep and essential insight into human nature. Therefore, for the first time in my life the existence of God in the world made its impact upon me as a positive and obtrusive fact.'

There was a famous correspondence in *The Times* 'What's wrong with the world?' Probably the most penetrating of all the letters was from G. K. Chesterton: 'Dear Sir, I am. Yours sincerely.' That is precisely the answer. The heart of the human problem is the problem of the human heart. People have a variety of theories about 'what is wrong with the world', but no one can truthfully answer this question until he can say with honesty 'Dear Sir, *I am*.' Christ described human nature in these words:

> 'From inside, out of a man's heart, come evil thoughts, acts of fornication, of theft, murder, adultery, ruthless greed and malice; fraud, indecency, envy, slander, arrogance, and folly; these evil things all come from inside, and they defile the man' (Mark 7.21–23 NEB).

Paul summed it up with a quotation from the Old Testament: 'All have turned aside, together they have gone wrong; no one does good, not even one' (Romans 3.12). Here 'gone wrong' means 'gone sour', like milk, or bad, like fruit–become rotten or putrid. Paul is therefore saying that human nature on its own, without Christ, is corrupt and useless in the sight of God.

One aspect of man's nature is reflected in the widespread feeling today that we can play with God's gift of sex. 'Why shouldn't I go to bed with a girl if I want to?' is a question that I am often asked in university circles. The first answer to that question is: because you are not a self-created being, responsible only to yourself. You are created by God and responsible to God.

> 'We shall all stand before God's tribunal. For Scripture says, "As I live, says the Lord, to me every knee shall bow and every tongue acknowledge God". So, you see, each of us will have to answer for himself' (Romans 14. 10–12 NEB).

Any complicated piece of machinery has with it the maker's instructions, and if these are ignored, the user has only himself to blame if things go wrong. God's laws are our Maker's instructions; we cannot toss them on one side as irrelevant nonsense without suffering the consequences. Some try to do so, but often with tragic results.

That is what the woman of Samaria found; she played with sex, and ignored her Maker's instructions. But her pursuit of happiness left her unhappy and dissatisfied.

Frustrated

In the second place, *her pursuit of freedom left her bound and enslaved to a way of life from which she many times longed to be free.* There is an extremely revealing comment on this woman's life. Christ exposes her sordid sex life, and she goes away to tell her friends: 'Come, see a man who told me *all that I ever did.*' Yet Christ had only talked about her abortive and miserable relationships with men. In other words, this *was* her life, and she was enslaved to it. In one way or another this enslavement is what always happens. We never find the freedom we want until we find it in Jesus Christ. Freedom, apart from Him, is a pure myth and delusion.

Ask the prodigal son: a man fed up with the stuffy rules of his father's house; who rebelled in order to be independent and free. It is worth looking at this story for a moment.[1] The son tells his father that it is time for him to leave; so he takes his inheritance and goes on his way to lead his life and spend his money and waste his time, just as he wants, in his own way. The father says not a word, and lets his son go. What does the young man find in this bid for freedom? Much the same as the Samaritan woman. But there are three disturbing factors as the weeks and months go by.

First, he can never quite get out of his mind the memory of

[1] Cf. Luke 15.11 f.

his father. He keeps on hearing his voice, seeing his face, and remembering his grief when he left home. He cannot quite free himself from these pricks of conscience. There is no silencer for the conscience on the market. Kafka, whom W. H. Auden insists is the most representative writer of the twentieth century, brings out in his novels *The Trial* and *The Castle* the fear of guilty man in relation to God. At one moment we desire to find God; in the next, we try to flee from Him. We protest violently that we want to be left alone, and yet being left alone is the very thing we most dread. In his love God will not leave us alone without doing His utmost to reach us. In Francis Thompson's famous words in *The Hound of Heaven:*

> *'I fled Him, down the nights and down the days;*
> *I fled Him, down the arches of the years;*
> *I fled Him, down the labyrinthine ways*
> *Of my own mind; and in the midst of tears*
> *I hid from Him, and under running laughter.'*

It is quite impossible to run away from God or to hide from His presence; wherever we are, He can reach us through our conscience, and our conscience always stays with us, whether we like it or not. But the young prodigal does not stop to think about that.

Secondly, he cannot get away from the fact that everything he has—clothes, food, money, possessions—comes from his father. The trouble is that he is trying to live his life without any reference to his father at all, and this spoils everything he does. He goes out to parties, but they do not satisfy him. He has a free and easy time with girls, but they give no lasting pleasure. He makes many friends, but they turn out to be fair-weather friends. That is always the trouble when we live in God's world without reference to God, and use His gifts without reference to the Giver. It does not and cannot satisfy: life becomes hollow and empty and pointless. But the young man does not stop to think about that.

Thirdly, he is not quite as free as he had imagined. He is gripped by boredom, and therefore must amuse himself. He is ruled by his natural desires, and therefore must indulge them. He is bound by the opinion of others, by the longing for popularity, by the fear of what others think; and therefore he must do this and that and the other. He is not free at all! Part One of the story of the prodigal ends with the young man penniless, starving, sitting in a pigsty feeding the pigs.

When a person tries to run away from God, he throws away the real potentiality that God has given him.

Paul says of those who could have found God but who turned away from Him: 'God gave them up to their own lusts...God gave them up to their own dishonourable passions...God gave them up to a base mind' (Romans 1.24, 26, 28). In the end, God did not run after them, but underlined their own decision and 'gave them up'. George Macdonald has said: 'The one principle of hell is—"I am my own".'

Christ once said 'Every one who commits sin' (that is, goes his own way, not God's, in his pursuit of freedom) 'is a slave to sin' (John 8.34). That is true, although it is part of the wretched deceitfulness of sin that a person may not realize how captive he is until there are crises. A sick person occasionally has an unnatural sense of well-being—*euphoria*. There is also such a thing as spiritual euphoria. Martin Luther, in his book *Bondage of the Will*, writes: 'Scripture sets before us a man who is not only bound, wretched, captive, sick and dead, but who, through the operation of Satan, his lord, adds to his other miseries that of blindness, so that he believes himself to be free, happy, possessed of liberty and ability, whole and alive.'

The Samaritan woman, as she talked with Jesus, began to discover the truth of these words. Jesus said to her, 'Every one who drinks of this water will thirst again' (John 4.13). Yes, she said to herself, this is just like my life: always needing further excitement, always wanting another kick, every day looking for something to satisfy my thirst. That was her second sad surprise: her pursuit of freedom left her enslaved to her desires, always seeking for fresh satisfaction.

Cut off

Her situation could be summarized by her third painful discovery. *Her pursuit of life ended up with mere existence.* She existed physically, but she did not live. She missed altogether the quality of life that God had planned for her. Many people, even famous people with astonishing success in the

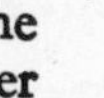

eyes of the world, have at the end of their lives had the humility to realize that without Christ they have simply existed and never lived. Darwin eventually confessed that by concentrating on only one aspect of life he had lost the power to enjoy poetry and music, and even nature itself. H. G. Wells, having rejected the Christian faith and worked out his own philosophy, admitted that he was utterly baffled and bewildered. His last book, significantly, was called *Mind at the End of its Tether*, and in this he says, '*Homo sapiens* is played out'. A spiritual rebel, despite every apparent promise of happiness, freedom and life, will always find himself cut off from God, the only Person who really loves and cares. That is the measure of his success.

Christ Relevant

What is Christ's relevance in such a situation? After His meeting with her the Samaritan woman could have given us the answer with considerable conviction.

Christ came first of all *not with condemnation or judgment: He came to satisfy and to save.* 'For God sent the Son into the world, not to condemn the world, but that the world might be saved through him' (John 3.17). Of course, there is condemnation and judgment for those who do not want the help that Christ offers. Tragically, the prevailing attitude today is that of sheer apathy. 'Why should I bother?' 'What's the point?' 'Why all the fuss?' This is the answer that the Bible gives: 'This is the judgment' (this is the condemning factor which brings the full wrath of God's judgment) 'that the light has come into the world, and men loved darkness rather than light' (John 3.19). In other words, they said 'Why bother?' Now that is the condemnation! 'He who does not believe is condemned already, because he has not believed in the name of the only Son of God (John 3.18). A person does not have to be against God before he is in danger of judgment. He simply has to be apathetic: 'I don't greatly care. I'm not honestly bothered. I can get on very well without your help, thank you very much—although, of course, when I am in difficulties I may pray to you, and I shall expect you to rush to my aid.' *That* is the condemnation, says Christ: treating God as your servant.

However, at His first approach Christ came without a note

of condemnation, and we see something far more remarkable than a Jewish rabbi talking with a Samaritan woman. We see the Son of God, caring for a sinner, a rebel. Why should *He* bother? That is a question we can never answer. We have gone our own way and broken His commandments and have not cared about Him. Why should He bother with any of us? But the fact is that He does!

Christ came, secondly, *not with a dreary set of religious rules, but with life;* 'Whoever drinks of the water that I shall give him will never thirst; the water that I shall give him will become in him a spring of water welling up to eternal life' (John 4.14). I find this wonderful! Eternal life is much more than life after death; it concerns life here and now. It means knowing Christ personally. In the story the woman was looking ahead to the dim and distant future: 'I know that Messiah is coming...when he comes, he will show us all things' (John 4.25). But Jesus cuts her short and talks about *now.* Christianity is not 'pie-in-the-sky-when-you-die'. Christ brings eternal life now. It is the quality of life that God longs for every person to have. It is like 'a spring of water welling up' inside: fresh, satisfying, quenching every thirst. No wonder the woman replied, 'Sir, give me this water, that I may not thirst'.

Christ came thirdly, *not with a big stick forcing her to obey, yet pressing the point as firmly as He could.* His tone was urgent. He longed to help this needy woman. God will never force a person to act, because He is a God of love and He wants a relationship of love. But while He comes gently and lovingly, He will still press a person hard, because love is urgent, love cares. C. S. Lewis describes this well when he recounts his conversion: 'I had always wanted above all things, not to be "interfered with". I had wanted (mad wish) "to call my soul my own".'

However, God is His love pursued him. He felt

> 'the steady unrelenting approach of Him whom I so earnestly desired not to meet. That which I greatly feared had at last come upon me. In the Trinity Term of 1929 I gave in, and admitted that God was God, and knelt and prayed: perhaps, that night, the most dejected and reluctant convert in all England. I did not then see what is now the most shining and obvious thing: the divine humility which will accept a convert

> even on such terms. The prodigal son at least walked home on his own feet. But who can duly adore that Love which will open the high gates to a prodigal who is brought in kicking, struggling, resentful and darting his eyes in every direction for a chance of escape? The words "compel them to come in" have been so abused by wicked men that we shudder at them; but properly understood they plumb the depth of the divine mercy.'[1]

If an individual feels Christ's compulsion like that, it is because the Saviour longs that he should know the freedom and liberation that He alone can bring.

Finally, Christ brought to the Samaritan woman *not a conventional religious life, but a challenge to be a rebel for Christ's sake.* She had a theological problem (although with her as with many it was far more a theological red herring to stave off the real challenge): 'Our fathers worshipped on this mountain; and you say that in Jerusalem is the place where men ought to worship'. 'No!' Jesus said, in effect, 'don't worry about where you ought to worship. You must worship the Father in spirit and in truth. It is a great spiritual adventure. You can go out every day in touch with your Heavenly Father. He's got plans for you, a job for you. It's exciting, it's life!' And at once she acted. She put her trust in Jesus and then raced off to find her friends, shouting 'Come, see a man...' And they came and they, too, believed. She was already finding the new life that Christ had brought; and it was exhilarating.

[1] C. S. Lewis: *Surprised by Joy* (Geoffrey Bles, 1967), p 182 f

and stabbing pains. And then came that shattering cry. One thing is certain: Christ's death is far more than a mere example of how to suffer. Indeed, if He died only as an example, we should not be impressed. Thousands of Christian martyrs have shown tremendous joy and ecstasy at the moment of their death. Thomas Bilney, for example, burnt at the stake in 1531, cried out until he died, 'Jesus, I believe! Jesus, I believe! Jesus, I believe!' Yet Jesus Himself cried, 'My God, my God, why has thou forsaken me?' Was He a coward and failure at the last moment? Surely not.

Further, it is totally inadequate to say that Christ died on the cross simply to win our love and allegiance. If someone showed his love for me by jumping into the sea and drowning, I should not be very impressed. In fact, like William Miller, we could only interpret this as 'the most pernicious form of emotional blackmail'. But Christ was doing something far more important than parading His love or demanding ours; He was suffering on that cross a torment which no other martyr could ever endure. He was bearing our sins. He endured, to use one unfashionable word, hell. We cannot begin to imagine what it could mean for God the Father and God the Son, perfectly united for all eternity, suddenly to be separated by the ugly black cloud of sin. That is what happened. In seven stark monosyllables Paul wrote that God 'made Him to be sin for us' (2 Corinthians 5.21 AV).

Sidney Carter, in his song *Friday Morning*, has very well expressed the confusion about the cross that is common today. Here are two verses, with one of the thieves speaking.

> '*It was on a Friday Morning*
> *That they took me from the cell,*
> *And I saw they had a carpenter*
> *To crucify as well.*
> *You can blame it on Pilate*
> *You can blame it on the Jews*
> *You can blame it on the Devil,*
> *It's God I accuse.*
> *It's God they ought to crucify*
> *Instead of you and me,*
> *I said to the carpenter*
> *A-hanging on the tree.*

'Now Barabbas was a killer
And they let Barabbas go.
But you are being crucified
For nothing here below.
But God is up in heaven
And he doesn't do a thing;
With a million angels watching
And they never move a wing.
It's God they ought to crucify
Instead of you and me,
I said to the carpenter
A-hanging on the tree.'

And the astonishing biblical revelation is this: It *was* God they crucified! 'God was in Christ reconciling the world to himself' (2 Corinthians 5.19). God the Father and God the Son are one. You cannot separate them–except on the cross, when Jesus became sin in our place, as our substitute.

The second cry from the cross which may help us to understand the heart of the matter is His last but one. 'It is finished!' In the Greek it is one word, *tetelesthai.* It has been called 'The greatest single word ever uttered'. What did Christ mean by this? Was He saying, pathetically, 'I am finished'? No! It says, 'Jesus cried with a loud voice'. It was a cry of triumph. Finished! Accomplished! The very purpose for which He had come into the world was now fulfilled. The same word was sometimes stamped across bills in those days, and simply means 'paid'. The transaction was finished, completed: there was nothing more to pay.

In the church in York where I am a minister, a tablet commemorates a Canon Faussett who, like a number of clergy of his day, owned land in Ireland. I am told that during one of the potato famines some families on his estate were unable to pay their rents, and wrote, begging him to let them off. He replied that he could not possibly do this: it was wrong, a bad precedent, and he could not possibly make an exception. They must pay their bills to the last penny. However, he enclosed with the letter a slip of paper. It was a cheque, for more than sufficient to cover all that they owed. That is just a tiny picture of what God accomplished in Christ on the cross, in order that we might be forgiven and that His justice might be satisfied.

Paul said to those who had given themselves to Christ:

'You.. God made alive.. having forgiven us all our trespasses, having cancelled the bond which stood against us with its legal demands; this he set aside, nailing it to the cross' (Colossians 2.13–14).

It was common practice to nail to the cross of a criminal an account of the crime that he had committed. But nailed to the cross of Christ, what do we find? An account of your sins and mine!

'It was my pride and hardness that nailed Him to the tree;
Those cruel nails, O Saviour, were driven in by me.'

In some deep and thoughtful words of Emil Brunner:

'In the Cross of Christ God says to man, "That is where you ought to be. Jesus My Son hangs there in your stead. His tragedy is the tragedy of your life. You are the rebel who should be hanged on the gallows. But lo, I suffered instead of you, and because of you, because I love you in spite of what you are. My love for you is so great that I meet you there, there on the cross. I cannot meet you anywhere else. You must meet Me there by identifying yourself with the One on the Cross. It is by this identification that I, God, can meet you in Him, saying to you as I say to Him, My beloved Son."

No wonder Paul said, "God forbid that I should boast of anything but the cross of our Lord Jesus Christ".

In the Gospel records, there was a strange and remarkable sign which accompanied this cry from the cross: we are told that the veil in the temple was torn in two from the top to the bottom. By itself this seems to be an extraordinary comment. The veil was a vast curtain separating the Holy of Holies (where God was said to dwell especially) from the rest of the building, and no one could pass through it except the high priest, once a year, with a blood sacrifice. This veil, of course, was a gigantic visual aid, a 'No Entry' sign. It represented the barrier of sin between the people and God. It was a constant reminder that God is holy, and that man cannot saunter into His presence with his hands in his pockets and his life full of sin. Voltaire once said, 'Of course God forgives sin; that's His business'. But there is no 'of course' anywhere in the New Testament. The tremendous Christian revelation is that God can forgive sin, but only through the cross of Jesus Christ.

Many people are only too conscious of this barrier between themselves and God. Prayer means little or nothing to them. The Bible seems a closed book. God is far away, remote and unreal. Isaiah gives the reason for this predicament: 'Your iniquities have made a separation between you and your God, and your sins have hid his face from you so that he does not hear' (59.2). Here is the curtain or barrier of sin. But when Christ died on that cross and when He cried out 'Finished!' the curtain in the temple was torn down. Nothing could have signified more clearly to any Jewish observer that the way into God's presence was now open.

Too good to be true?

Further, it is important to realize that the cross of Christ is completely *sufficient for the sin* of man. 'Christ also died for our sins once and for all', said Peter (1 Peter 3.18). Although the cross happened at a moment in history, it has eternal significance. However, in my experience, there are various deep-rooted questions which are asked repeatedly.

'*Is there any other way to God and to heaven?*' In these days of multi-faith services, the implication is that all roads lead to God, and it does not greatly matter which road you travel on, provided that you are sincere. The answer to this question is clear. If we can get to heaven by good works, why did Christ bother to come into this world at all? If it is possible to be accepted by God through a decent life, why did Christ bother to die? If we can earn forgiveness by being religious, why did Christ bother to suffer the torments of hell? If we can do it by our own efforts, why did Christ bother?

There is no other way to God except by Jesus Christ and on the grounds of His death on the cross. Christ Himself said, 'No one comes to the Father, but by me'. Peter said, 'There is salvation in no one else, for there is no other name under heaven given among men, by which we must be saved'. Paul said, 'There is one mediator between God and men, the man Christ Jesus, who gave himself as a ransom for all' (John 14.6; Acts 4.12; 1 Timothy 2.5–6).

This last quote is especially interesting. In Athens, in those days, if two parties had a quarrel they would present their case to a body of men called 'The Forty'. The Forty would then appoint a mediator, whose task was clearly defined: he must faithfully represent both parties, and then bring them together whatever the cost might be to himself. In spiritual terms, Christ alone has represented both the parties of God and man: He alone was both God and man. He alone is the bridge which touches both sides, and He has brought us to God at the infinite cost of His own blood shed on the cross. There is no other way to God at all.

'*Does it really matter?*' Briefly, there is no greater proof of the reality of God's judgment than the cross itself. See Christ's agony, look at the horror of it all, hear that cry of dereliction. There is the reality of judgment! Christ has died to save us from that judgment, but there is a question that no one can answer: 'How shall we escape if we neglect such a great salvation?' (Hebrew 2.3).

'*Can I come to Christ when I want to?*' It is a surprisingly common fallacy that we can treat God, perhaps unconsciously, as our servant, ready at our beck and call. When the convenient moment comes (if it ever does), then we can say to Him, 'All right, I am ready for you now. You can come into my life if you want to.' The Bible makes it quite clear who is the Master and who is the servant. 'Seek the Lord while he may be found, call upon him while he is near' (Isaiah 55.6). He is not always to be found; He is not always near. Therefore when He is, it is essential that we take the opportunity while we have it. God's time is always now. 'Today, when you hear his voice, do not harden your hearts' (Hebrews 3.7–8). If we do not act when we hear God's voice, then we do harden our hearts, and we stand in grave danger of never hearing God's voice again.

'*But I could never keep it up.*' This is a common fear. Briefly, the answer is: no, you could never keep it up; but Christ can keep you up. Jude says that He 'is able to keep you from falling' (v. 24). When you commit your life to Christ, the mighty Spirit of God comes to live in your inmost being. Therefore, you are able to do things which you could never do before. You live the Christian life—with His help! You cannot trust Him too much for His courage, His guidance, His love to cast out your fears, His power over temptation and sin.

'*Is there anything for me to do?*' In one sense the answer to that is, No. Everything has been done for us, because Christ has borne our sins once and for all. It is finished! Therefore He offers a free gift, which we simply have to accept. 'The free gift of God is eternal life in Christ Jesus our Lord' (Romans 6.23).

A young boy once sat down with pencil and paper. He wrote down all the sins that were on his conscience: a long and miserable list. Then he took a match and set light to the paper. As he watched the flames burn up the paper he said to himself, 'Christ died for my sins'. And as the breeze blew the ashes into the air he added, 'And he carried my sins right away'. That is the assurance that every Christian can and should have.

CHAPTER FIVE

The Resurrection— Christ our Contemporary?

'Why is there so little evidence?' Often I am asked that question. 'If this Christian gospel is really true, as you Christians claim; if a belief in Jesus Christ is vital; if my whole future destiny depends on my response to Christ here and now; if Christ is the Way, the Truth, and the Life, and no one comes to the Father but by Him, then why is there so little evidence? Why isn't God more convincing? Why doesn't He help us to believe?'

Causes of Doubt

It is important here to look briefly at the whole question of doubt. Jesus said, in a passage referring to His resurrection, 'Be unbelieving no longer' (John 20.27 NEB). The cause of doubt is not always lack of evidence. There may be plenty of evidence, and yet people doubt. What are the main reasons?

There are few more relevant characters in the New Testament than Thomas the doubter. Today he is probably the most widely accepted patron saint! Now there is something likeable about Thomas: he was absolutely down-to-earth and practical, and he was very honest in his doubts. He refused to say he believed when he frankly did not.

But Thomas had several problems. *He was a pessimist.* When Jesus talked about going back into Judaea, where he was likely to face hot opposition, Thomas, in his typical frame of mind, said 'Let us also go, that we may die with him' (John 11.16). He was always fearing the worst, always looking on the gloomy side of things. Many are held back from a real faith in Christ for precisely the same reason. One part of them wants to believe, another says 'What about my friends? What about my marriage? What about my career? This won't last.' Thus, they are hindered from a true belief in Christ by fear, or sheer pessimism.

Again, Thomas was *a sceptic.* He was over-cautious when he should have believed. Go back to that first Easter Day, and imagine him passing through the dark streets of Jerusalem to the house where the disciples have met together. He is still downcast and sad after the terrible events of the last few days. He comes to the house, knocks on the door, and steps in. All at once he is surrounded by excitement. 'Thomas, we have seen the Lord! We have seen the Lord!' Here are ten Apostles, together with an unknown number of other disciples: all mature, honest and reliable; and all saying with tremendous enthusiasm, 'We've seen the Lord!' But Thomas replies, 'Unless I see in his hands the print of the nails, and place my finger in the mark of the nails, and place my hand in his side, I will not believe' (John 20.25). The force of the original is not 'When I see...I will believe', but 'Unless I see... I won't believe'. Why not, Thomas? 'Because I don't understand it and they might possibly be wrong.'

Logically, that is true. But a person will never resolve his doubts if he considers all the logically possible alternatives to faith, or if he waits until he understands it all. How dreary! Where is the adventure of faith? Without this adventure there would be no discoveries: no knowledge of anything, not even of science, and certainly not of God. Confucius said, 'If men spoke only of those things of which they have knowledge, the world would be full of long and majestic silences'.

Thomas was also *disillusioned.* He and the others had pinned their hopes and staked their lives on Jesus Christ. But after all those shattering events, leading up to the crucifixion, they were all terribly disillusioned.

I am constantly meeting people who are disillusioned by what they have seen of the Christian faith in the past. Sandie Shaw once remarked, 'I don't go to church. Well, I mean, you meet such cranky people who do! Church seems to attract them. I'm sure Christianity was all right in the beginning, but not now!' C. S. Lewis made the same complaint, although perhaps in a more sophisticated style:

> 'Though I liked clergymen as I liked bears, I had as little wish to be in the Church as in the zoo. It was, to begin with...a wearisome "get-together" affair . . . the fussy time-wasting botheration of it all! The bells, the crowds, the umbrellas, the notices, the bustle, the perpetual arranging and organizing.

Hymns were (and are) extremely disagreeable to me. Of all musical instruments, I liked (and like) the organ least.'[1]

In 1966 Lord Eccles wrote his book *Half Way to Faith*. Lord Eccles, brought up in the formal and forbidding atmosphere of conventional Christianity, is a confessed unbeliever:

> 'My doubts were increased by the difficulty I had to recognize a professing Christian by his behaviour. I looked round among my believing friends and acquaintances for signs if their faith influenced their conduct. Perhaps I had bad luck, for the experiment was a failure, and what made it particularly depressing was that some of the most unselfish and honourable men, had, as far as I could tell, no religion in them, and certainly never went to church except as a social function' (p 57).

Further, he clearly received little help from those responsible for his Christian instruction. Concerning an artist whom he admired, he wrote:

> 'He showed me that if I loved a picture at first sight I should afterwards gain a much more valuable understanding of it, than if I had looked at it without emotion, pulled it to pieces and analysed it with all the apparatus of scholarship to help me. He proved to me that love comes first and understanding second. But no one translated this experience into the categories of religion. No one suggested that perhaps this was also the first step towards the knowledge of God' (p 24).

That is a very shrewd remark. In all deep personal relationships, '*love comes first and understanding second*'. Many people ask far too many questions about the Christian faith. 'When I understand, then I'll believe.' But God says, 'No: believe—and then you will begin to understand'. However, many feel that they simply cannot believe because of the disillusionment they have experienced over the years.

There is, of course, a most important distinction to be borne in mind. Religion and true Christianity are not necessarily the same thing. Neither are nominal Christians and committed Christians to be thought of as the same. Again, the visible congregation and the invisible Church are likely to be different: Christ warned us about this when He said that

[1] *Surprised by Joy* (Fontana), p 187

within the visible Church there would be both wheat and weeds growing together until the Day of Judgment.[1] Unfortunately many cannot distinguish the wheat from the weeds. Much of our church life today is certainly a travesty of the teaching of Jesus Christ: full of formality, snobbery and hypocrisy; rejecting the commandments of God in favour of the traditions of men; petty minded, and often ignoring the real needs of the world. This is just what Christ said of the religious leaders of His day. To be disillusioned about these things, however, is no reason for doubting the truth and reality of Christ Himself.

Another cause for unbelief is superficial judgment. In his booklet *Unbelief to Faith*,[2] Stuart Mawson, a Harley Street surgeon, recalls how he came up to Cambridge University and 'began to taste the heady wine of intellectual freedom'. He rebelled against the rules of chastity and the authority of religion; and putting his Bible away, he turned his back on the Church, and 'passionately embraced the "grown up" philosophy of scientific humanism'. And there he stayed throughout his university career and for many years afterwards, convinced 'that the glory of man lay in his courage and determination to make the best of things'.

However, as he became more mature he came to appreciate the limitations of science. You could not measure the love between a man and a woman, or the spirit in a football team; and just possibly the same was true of God Himself, if He existed at all. Not everything in life could be reduced to the terms of logic and science. Mawson realized that the scientific method had always been to experiment, and not to rely on the second-hand opinions of others, and therefore, he planned an experiment in the realm of Christian faith. He determined to test Christianity for a whole year to see what it really contained. He soon discovered that he had a deep-rooted prejudice against Christians in general and clergymen in particular! This he felt was basically irrational, but real. Then he took serious measures to investigate Christian belief, and found, to his surprise, that it had a sound intellectual basis. Intellectually it was just as possible to believe as not to believe. It was true that sitting in an armchair one could not

[1] Matthew 13.24–30 [2] IVP, 1958

prove Christianity, but neither could one disprove it. So the pursuit went on.

Six months went by, but there was no further progress because he had not yet grasped the fact that if God is a person He must be known as a person, experimentally, in a dynamic way. Eventually he came to see that God could be known in Jesus Christ. And the culminating point in his experiment came when deliberately, thoughtfully, trustingly and wholeheartedly he committed his life to Christ. He felt like a scientist on the threshold of a new discovery, not knowing what to expect, and possibly about to make a fool of himself. Christ honoured that experiment. He promises, 'Seek, and you will find'. Here was a man who sought, and he did find. He found Christ to be real and living, and utterly true to His word. He is one of countless Christians who know the reality of Christ's resurrection in their own experience.

Fact or Fancy

This was the message that absolutely thrilled those first Christians: God had given them overwhelming proof that Jesus Christ was what He claimed to be. His teaching was unsurpassed; His character was a miracle; but God had set His final seal by raising Him from the dead! They knew it to be true. The evidence was indisputable. It was a glorious historical fact. And, as Professor J. N. D. Anderson has pointed out, this message is 'Either the supreme fact in history or else a gigantic hoax'.

One question, before we go any further: how important is it to believe in a literal resurrection of Jesus Christ from the dead? For some this is an immense supernatural barrier. Christian morality is all very well; being kind, forgiving, generous and thoughtful is good common sense. But why bring in the supernatural? Why introduce the very things which might prove a stumbling-block to the rationalist and scientist? Why not present the resurrection as a beautiful story—a parable, a metaphor, an illustration, teaching profound truth but not literally true? This is clearly a popular view today.

Paul knew the answer to that one: 'If Christ has not been raised [literally] then our preaching is in vain...we are... misrepresenting God...your faith is futile...you are still in your sins...those also who have fallen asleep in Christ have perished...we are of all men most to be pitied' (1 Corinthians 15.14–19).

One man who saw this very clearly a little while ago, was a retired clergyman. During his retirement he read various books on the New Theology, and watched a number of television discussions on the subject of the resurrection. In his old age he felt sure that these highly qualified writers and speakers knew far more than he did, and that when they said there was no literal resurrection of Christ, they must surely be right. That is what he felt. The only trouble was that he knew exactly what this meant. His whole Christian life and ministry had been based on nothing more than a bundle of myths. Fairy tales! He committed suicide. The famous Bible translator, J. B. Phillips, heard about the suicide and, full of righteous anger, sat down and wrote his book *Ring of Truth*. In the foreword he says:

> 'For many years it has been my solid purpose to communicate the truth of the Christian gospel. I am not concerned to distort or dilute the Christian faith so that modern undergraduates, for example, can accept it without a murmur. I am concerned with the truth revealed in and through Jesus Christ... I do not care a rap what the "avant-garde" scholars say; I do very much care what God says and does. I have therefore felt compelled to write this book. It is my testimony to the historicity and reliability of the New Testament.'[1]

J. B. Phillips, of course, has spent all his life in studying and translating the New Testament. For him the resurrection is a plain, literal, historical fact.

What then is the evidence? We must remember that the New Testament records were written by men whose honesty and integrity stand out a mile. They risked their necks by proclaiming the truth, with great boldness, before the very city crowds which a few weeks before had murdered their Master: 'God has made him both Lord and Christ, this Jesus whom you crucified'; 'God...raised Jesus whom you killed' (Acts 2.36; 5.30). Naturally they suffered for their boldness. They were imprisoned and beaten, Stephen was killed by stoning, James by the sword. The rulers, we are told, were

[1] J. B. Phillips: *Ring of Truth* (Hodder and Stoughton, 1967)

'sawn asunder with rage' by their preaching. Could this possibly have been the context of a stupendous hoax?

However, we must look at the facts themselves. There are three outstanding ones.

The Empty Tomb

It is almost impossible to try to recapture the scene of that first Easter morning. Without any doubt the Apostles had been crushed by the shattering events of the crucifixion. Jesus was dead and buried, finished and gone. They had not the slightest ray of hope to dispel their gloom; not the faintest suggestion that somehow, some time, Jesus would rise from the dead. Indeed, the Gospel records make it perfectly clear that when the first disciples came back with the astonishing news that the tomb was empty and Jesus alive, the others would not believe it: 'idle talk', they called it. Nevertheless, the fact remained that the tomb was empty. At least five disciples saw it early that Easter morning, and soon it was common knowledge. Further, those first disciples saw the linen cloths lying on the slab where the body should have been, the linen cloths which had been wrapped round the body lying there, undisturbed–but no body.

Now anyone who argues against the Resurrection has to find a satisfactory answer to the question, 'what had happened to the body'? There have been plenty of suggestions.

The disciples stole it. But would they honestly have taken the naked body of their Master? Would they really have been so skilful in their deception that the body was never found (notoriously difficult), with the result that they and many of their friends suffered martyrdom, for what they knew all along was a lie? Is there a 'ring of truth' about that?

The Jewish or Roman authorities stole it. What motive would they have had? They had sealed the tomb and set a guard on it to ensure that the body would not be stolen. They were of course, fanatically opposed to the preaching of the resurrection; so that if they had had the body, they had a trump card to silence the disciples once and for all. But no body could they produce.

Tomb robbers stole it. They were common enough at that time; but what thief would deliberately and carefully leave behind the grave clothes, together with a hundred pounds of precious spices, by far the most valuable possession of the whole tomb?

Jesus never died. He simply fainted, according to this theory, recovered in the cool restfulness of the tomb and escaped from it to show Himself as a 'risen' Lord and Master. Is that really possible? Can we possibly believe that a man who staggered on his way to Calvary, hung nailed to the cross for six hours, lost consciousness and then was placed in a stone tomb for three days without food or medical attention, could then revive? Can we accept that in this desperate situation he could escape from his grave clothes and roll back the heavy stone which three women feared was beyond their strength to move, and then walk for miles on lacerated feet? Is that really possible? Even the sceptic Strauss makes the comment:

> 'It is impossible that a being who had stolen half dead out of the sepulchre, who crept about weak and ill, wanting medical treatment, who required bandaging, strengthening, and indulgence, who still at last yielded to His sufferings, could have given the disciples the impression that He was a conqueror over death and the grave, the Prince of Life.'

And would Christ, of all people, have created such a monstrous fraud as that?

None of these theories begins to do any justice to the plain facts.

Resurrection appearances

Christ afterwards showed Himself to the disciples on at least ten separate occasions, scattered over a period of six weeks. He was seen in many places: by the tomb, on the road to Emmaus, in the Upper Room, by the Sea of Galilee, on the hills, in Jerusalem, and on the Mount of Olives. What was it that so completely convinced Simon Peter and turned that utter sorrow after his denial into those forthright and startling declarations on the day of Pentecost? Paul tells us: the risen Christ appeared to him (1 Corinthians 15.5). What was it that so convinced James, the Lord's brother, when he did not believe during Christ's life and ministry? Again, Paul says that the risen Christ appeared to him (1 Corinthians 15.7). What was it that so convinced doubting Thomas, full of demands for visible, tangible proof, pessimistic, sceptical, disbelieving? The risen Christ appeared to him (John 20.24–8). What was it that so persuaded Saul of Tarsus, number one arch-enemy of the Church? The answer is the same: he himself tells us that the risen Christ appeared to him also (1 Corinthians 15.8).

A critic may say, if he likes, that they were all in a highly emotional state, easy prey to some form of hallucination. But is that likely to have been true? A materialist like Thomas? A hard-headed business man like Matthew? An intelligent doctor like Luke? Down-to-earth, tough fishermen like Andrew, Peter, James and John? A brilliant scholar like Paul? 'Highly emotional'? This would be a monstrous misinterpretation of historical facts!

There was in the appearance of Jesus nothing resembling an hallucination. He could be seen, heard and touched. He could walk. He could show the marks of His sufferings. He could cook fish, and even eat it.

Moreover, Paul tells us that the risen Christ was on one occasion seen by more than five hundred people at once, most of whom were still alive when he wrote and could vouch for the truth of his statement. My first Vicar, on the Easter Day after my ordination, did an unusual thing. When he mounted the pulpit to preach his sermon, before uttering a word, he solemnly took a daffodil from a vase by the pulpit, and proceeded to eat it, flower, stalk and all, in front of the congregation! Then he said something like this: 'Suppose you were to go out of the church at the end of the service, and see a man on the other side of the street who had not been here. Suppose you went up to him and said, "The Vicar did a most extraordinary thing this morning. He ate a flower in the pulpit!" Suppose the man said, "I don't believe you. I know the Vicar, and he would never do a thing like that!" Then suppose that a second person came out of church and said exactly the same thing to this man. And then a third, and then a fourth. There must be about two hundred and fifty people in church this morning. The man would be very foolish indeed if he did not believe that this incident occurred after having heard two hundred and fifty people describe it.

Far more impressive, over five hundred people saw Jesus at one time, and could testify to the truth of what Paul was saying, that Christ was and is alive!'

Sir Edward Clarke, KC, wrote:

> 'As a lawyer, I have made a prolonged study of the evidence for the events of the first Easter Day. To me the evidence is conclusive, and over and over again in the High Court, I have secured the verdict on evidence not nearly so compelling . . . As a lawyer, I accept (the Gospel evidence for the Resurrection) unreservedly as the testimony of truthful men to facts that they were able to substantiate.'[1]

Tolkien, in his book *Tree and Leaf*, says that the resurrection story

> 'Has pre-eminently the "inner consistency of reality". There is no tale ever told that men would rather find was true and none which so many sceptical men have accepted as true on its own merits . . . To reject it leads either to sadness or to wrath.'

In 1930 one sceptic, Frank Morison, set out to write a book disproving the resurrection as a groundless myth. But the more he studied the Gospel records, the more he was shaken in his original intention, and the more he was convinced that in fact the resurrection did happen. The book he wrote was very different from the one he had originally planned. It is called *Who Moved the Stone*?[2] and the opening chapter is entitled 'The book that refused to be written'. In the following chapters he goes on to explain 'Why that other venture never came to port, what were the hidden rocks upon which it foundered, and how I landed upon, to me, an unexpected shore'–the shore of certainty that Jesus was and is alive.

The Witness of the Holy Spirit

Christ had told His disciples that after His resurrection and ascension He would not leave them alone and helpless, but that He would give them the gift and power of God's Holy Spirit. He told them to wait in Jerusalem until this promise had been fulfilled and the gift given, and it is obvious that at

[1] Quoted by J. R. W. Stott in *Basic Christianity* (I.V.P. 1958), p 46

[2] (Faber, paperback ed. 1965)

that moment the disciples had not the slightest wish to witness to Jesus. Indeed, they were timid, nervous and fearful. They were huddled together behind locked doors, full of fears and forebodings. They had no leader, no inspiration, no security–nothing! Never before had they been so absolutely overwhelmed by the feeling of helplessness.

But something happened which transformed the whole scene. The Spirit came upon them. The disciples were filled with power and boldness. Peter preached: three thousand people were converted. Everyone was filled with awe and many miracles were performed. A well-known cripple was completely healed. Peter preached again: 'You...killed the Author of life, whom God raised from the dead...Repent therefore...that your sins may be blotted out' (Acts 3.14–15, 19). Two thousand more were converted. The opposition grew. The disciples were threatened and beaten, one was killed, and then another. But they forged ahead in the power of the Holy Spirit, all the time testifying that–Jesus was alive. Wherever they went they left abundant evidence that something very remarkable indeed had happened. So much so that a few years later, even their avowed opponents described them as 'these men who have turned the world upside down' (Acts 17.6).

What explanation is there for historical facts like these–for the birth and growth of the Christian Church? How are we to understand these lives which were totally transformed? Take the case of Simon Peter: a craven coward when Jesus was arrested, but a little later frightened of nothing and no one! And what of the stories of others? The power and influence of Jesus Christ, in the world, century after century up to this present day, has been one of the greatest and most remarkable factors in the history of mankind. Today there are an estimated 950,000,000 believers.

Napoleon once said, with a characteristic blend of conceit and truth:

> 'An extraordinary power of influencing and commanding men has been given to Alexander, Charlemagne and myself. But with us, the presence has been necessary, the eye, the voice, the hands. Whereas Jesus Christ has influenced and commanded His subjects without visible bodily presence for eighteen hundred years.'

Sometimes the accusation is made, however, that although this evidence may sound very convincing, Christians are always appealing to the past. They go to the Bible and look at their New Testament. They talk about the events of two thousand years ago. They appeal to Church history, but it is always history. Where is the evidence today? If Jesus is alive today, why doesn't He show Himself?

Certainly Christians do go back to the past, because, unlike nearly all other philosophies and religions, Christianity is rooted in historical facts. However, there is plenty of evidence today. I have personally talked to thousands of men and women, from university professors to drug addicts, from top-class scientists to simple country folk: they all give the same evidence, that of the reality of Jesus Christ in their own lives and experience. In Chapter 7 I quote one or two examples.

In one of His most powerful parables, Christ declared that if a person will not accept the abundant evidence that God has given, then even 'if someone should rise from the dead' that person will still not believe! Many people have been honest enough to tell me that they do not believe because they do not want to believe.

However, there is one further piece of evidence about the resurrection of Christ that anyone can have. You can know Him yourself. You can find the living Christ in your own experience. You can conduct the sort of experiment that I mentioned earlier in this chapter.

Of course, if this evidence is false, then you must accept the only alternative conclusion: that the whole of Christianity is a complete and absolute fraud, a terrible deception—and that it has been so for two thousand years.

On the other hand, if this evidence is true (and I would suggest that the facts are conclusive), then it is of the utmost importance that each of us does something about it. Since Christ has risen from the dead, His teaching is true, there is life after death, there is judgment to come, there is a heaven, there is a hell, and Christ is the Son of God. Moreover, He gave this promise: 'I am the resurrection and the life; he who believes in me, though he die, yet shall he live' (John 11.25). We should notice carefully those words 'he who believes in me'. In the New Testament, *to believe* means *to commit oneself personally*. Therefore, our personal commitment to Christ now determines our whole destiny. No one can play with Jesus Christ. No one can keep Him at a distance for ever. One day we shall meet Him face to face, whether we like it or not, or whether we believe it now or not. At the name of Jesus every knee will bow and every tongue confess that He is Lord (Philippians 2.9–10), and on that day the great question will be: do you know Him personally? To many He will have to say with great sadness 'I never knew you: out of my sight!' (Matthew 7.23 NEB).

CHAPTER SIX

The Cost—No Life of My Own?

In this chapter I want to go one stage further, and make a sober estimate of what it means to become a true Christian. One answer is this: Christ becomes my friend, the greatest friend I could ever have. Now this is the whole purpose of our creation, that we should have a personal relationship with Christ. Until we see Christianity as a friendship with Jesus, we have not begun to understand the heart of it all. I remember what a relevation this was to me as an undergraduate at Cambridge. I had thought of Christianity as an outworn creed, a dreary set of rules, or the habit of church-going, but never realized that Christ wanted to become my own friend. And, indeed, it was not until I had committed my life to Him that I came to see what a wonderful friend He could be: a friend who loves and cares, who forgives time and time again, who understands our needs, who feels with us in times of suffering and temptation, who guides and leads, and who never leaves us, whatever may happen. A student at Cambridge said to me recently, 'Jesus is the one permanent object of our trust and affections, in an age that is shifting and temporary'.

One of the greatest compliments ever paid to Christ in the Gospels is that He was called 'a friend of sinners'. It was intended as an insult, but in fact it is a glorious truth. His love and compassion are such that He longs to be the friend of those who are breaking His laws and rebelling against Him. Therefore, if at this moment you want to have nothing to do with Christ, He still wants to be your friend! If you are determined to turn your back on Him and go your own way, Christ still wants to be your friend. If you are full of arguments and excuses why you don't believe and won't believe, Christ still wants to be your friend. If you are treating Him like a servant, keeping Him in reserve in case you may one day want Him, Christ still wants to be your friend. He is the friend of sinners.

Making an Estimate

In order that we might understand the cost clearly, I want to look at one young man who knew something of his need, and was considering seriously the whole question of his relationship with Christ (Matthew 19.16–22; Mark 10.17–22). He came one day and asked Jesus 'Good Teacher, what must I do to inherit eternal life?' We could say that he was wanting to make an estimate of what it meant to become a Christian.

Of the many individuals who met with Christ, this was one of the most likeable. Mark tells us that 'Jesus, looking upon him loved him'. There was something which especially warmed the heart of Christ when He saw this splendid young man. Here, surely, was the ideal disciple, one of the few with natural gifts of leadership and initiative: first-class material, someone who could carry the gospel into places of influence; perhaps even someone who could win leaders for Christ.

In a few strokes of the pen, we have a fairly impressive portrait of this young man. He was a *ruler*, which was roughly equivalent to a Member of Parliament in those days. He was *polite* and *respectful*. We see him kneeling before Jesus and calling Him 'Teacher'. Jesus, humanly speaking, was only a poor unknown carpenter's son from the insignificant town of Nazareth; a strange itinerant preacher. Yet here was this Member of Parliament kneeling and calling Him 'Good Teacher...Good Master'.

The young man was also *sincere* and *upright*. He claimed that he had observed the Commandments from childhood days, and I do not believe that this was a proud, vain boast, because humbly he went on to ask, 'What do I still lack?' He was ready to admit that he had still something to learn or do. Above all, he was *earnest* and *wise*. His earnestness can be seen in the fact that he publicly *ran* to Jesus and *knelt* before Him. His wisdom can be seen in the question he asked: 'What must I do to inherit eternal life?'

You can always tell a wise person, not primarily by the answers he gives, but by the questions he asks. So many today are asking the wrong questions: How can I earn more and work less? How can I be happy? How can I get on? How can I be successful, popular, pretty? These questions may be of some importance, but they are totally irrelevant compared to this first and foremost question about eternal life.

Eternal Life

What is eternal life? It is so easy for Christians to talk in pious phrases! Is it just singing praises in heaven year after year after year? A perpetual evening service? Even to the most heavenly minded person this would not seem an immensely attractive proposition! The essence of eternal life is its perfect quality, rather than its endless duration. (I am not at all sure that time means anything after death; it is purely a human limitation.) Therefore, eternal life means the life that Christ longs for us to have: 'I have come that men may have life, and may have it in all its fullness' (John 10.10 NEB). Eternal life begins now, as soon as a person finds Christ. It continues even more wonderfully after death.

Perhaps we can only begin to understand the true meaning of life when we have grasped something of the meaning of death. There are three forms of death, and the common factor in each is *separation*.

Physical death. The body is dead, and is separated both from the soul and from people still living on this earth.

Spiritual death. The soul is dead and is separated from God though the body is alive. This, of course, is something we all experience, until we come to Christ. Christ came to bring us to God: that was His great purpose, and the significance of His death and resurrection; and only by these can we have spiritual life, because by nature we are spiritually dead. Our soul is dead to God. Spiritual death is solemn enough; but at least we can do something about it here and now, by accepting Christ as our own Saviour.

Eternal death, when both body and soul are dead and separated from God for ever. And physical death seals our destiny once and for all. Jesus taught clearly that there is no second chance after death whatsoever. When I die physically, I am eternally either dead or alive; either separated from God with appalling finality, having to bear the full righteous judgment of God on my sin, or in the presence of God in a way that is unimaginably wonderful.

> 'Mankind is divided into the righteous and the wicked with no intermediate class. There is good and evil without any middle ground. There is light and darkness without any twilight. There is heaven and hell without any purgatory.

> Men must choose between life and death, between being saved or lost.[1]

We do not fully understand what it means to be lost, or to suffer eternal death. But you cannot escape the fact that Christ, who loved us and cared for us, deliberately chose the most solemn words and metaphors to describe the nature of hell.

Costly Mistakes

Coming back to the story, we can see the wisdom of this young man when he asked, 'What must I do to inherit eternal life?' He knew he was asking the one question of absolutely vital importance.

Nevertheless, this story is a tragic one: because the young man, although bursting with promise and potential, made three classic, common mistakes leading to disastrous results.

First, *he underestimated the Godhead of Christ*. 'Good Teacher!' he said: and Christ replied, 'Why do you call me good? No one is good but God alone.' In other words, the one conclusion you simply cannot make about Christ is that He is simply a 'Good Teacher'. (If you think I am only a teacher, Christ was saying to him, then I am not good in God's eyes. I am a sinner like you and like everyone else; and My advice is no better than anyone else's. On the other hand, if I really am good, you must conclude that I am God, because only God is good.) 'Good Teacher' is therefore an impossible description.[2] Certainly we need to remember this when we discuss the Christian faith and eternal life. We are discussing the teaching of God Himself.

Someone said to me, when talking about these things, 'I love a religious argument!' But I asked him, 'What is there to argue about? Do you know what happens beyond the grave? Do you know about eternal life and eternal death? Of course you don't!' Thomas and Philip were asking these questions one day. How can we know, they asked, that there is life after death? How can we know that God exists? Because unless we do know, the Christian life frankly is not worth it. To answer both these questions, Jesus pointed emphatically to Himself.

[1] J. Oswald Sanders: *What of the Unevangelized?* p 10
[2] See chapter 1 for a fuller argument.

Do you want to know the way to God, Thomas? 'I am the way, and the truth, and the life; no one comes to the Father, but by me.' Do you want to see the Father, Philip? 'He who has seen me has seen the Father.' In other words, if you want to know about God, and the things of God, said Jesus, you must come to Me, you must look to Me, you must listen to Me. Now that is a very daring thing to say, but again and again Christ spoke and lived 'as one having authority'. Repeatedly we find people holding their breath with astonishment at his words. They were amazed! 'No man ever spoke like this man!' (John 8.46). That was true.

Nor were His claims empty words. Both friend and foe were dumbfounded by the selfless, sinless life of Jesus. Constantly they were astonished as they saw lame men leaping to their feet, blind men seeing, deaf men hearing, the wind and the waves obeying His command. They heard Him forgive sins, and command the dead to rise. They even saw Him risen from the dead. Someone has said,

> 'I am far within the mark when I say that all the armies that ever marched, and all the navies that ever sailed, and all the parliaments that ever sat, and all the kings that ever reigned, put together have not affected the life of man upon earth as has that One Solitary Life.'

Moreover, His teaching is perfectly clear. You can open your New Testament and find it on page after page. You cannot push it on one side as irrelevant nonsense. Some try to do so: they give subtle interpretations of Scripture as they read between the lines. C. S. Lewis, in his book *Christian Reflections*, made this comment:

> 'This then is my first bleat. These men [liberal scholars] ask me to believe that they can read between the lines of the old texts; the evidence is their obvious inability to read (in any sense worth discussing) the lines themselves. They claim to see fern seed and can't see an elephant ten yards away in broad daylight' (p 157).

Therefore, if we approach Christ, like the young man in the story, assuming that He is just a good teacher, we are underestimating His Godhead and we are underestimating His authority. Concerning the supreme question of eternal life, God has spoken through His Son, Jesus Christ.

Then this young man made a second, common mistake: *he overestimated his own goodness.* 'What must *I do* to inherit eternal life?' It seems from the context that he felt, along with a great many others today, that somehow he could earn eternal life. It was almost within his grasp; he had kept the Commandments all his life, so what did he still lack? He obviously felt that he was 'almost there'. This is a terribly common misconception. Often I hear words like these. 'Surely God must accept me. I believe in Him, I do my best, I try hard, I sometimes pray and maybe even go to church. What more could He want?'

On 19th December 1923, Arthur Buller's famous limerick first appeared in *Punch:*

> '*There was a young lady named Bright,*
> *Whose speed was far faster than light;*
> *She set out one day*
> *In a relative way,*
> *And returned home the previous night.*'

This limerick, of course, was trying to capture the spirit of the age: that man was potentially, at least, master of his situation. If he had not yet conquered in every field of knowledge, the triumph was not so far away. Is man really master of his situation? Look at man himself: his nature, his human reactions to other human beings with similar natures and reactions. Lord Eccles writes,

> 'The multitude of new facts and theories does not help us to behave better. Indeed, mankind as a whole tells more lies... It seems that because it is easier to travel to the moon, it is harder to make men unselfish and truthful.'[1]

This is a shrewd and realistic assessment of the fact of human nature, a fact from which no one can escape, and I doubt if there is any doctrine more difficult to deny than the universality of sin. William Temple once said, speaking about Salvation, 'All is of God. The only thing of my very own which I contribute to my redemption is the sin from which I need to be redeemed!'

The young ruler underestimated the Godhead of Christ; he overestimated his own goodness; and because of these two

[1] Eccles: *Halfway to faith*, p 67.

errors, *he never estimated the cost of discipleship.* To quote C. S. Lewis again, in *Mere Christianity:*

> 'When I was a child I often had toothache, and I knew that if I went to my mother, she would give me something which would deaden the pain for that night and let me get to sleep. But I did not go to my mother–at least not until the pain became very bad. And the reason why I did not go was this. I did not doubt that she would give me the aspirin; but I knew she would also do something else. I knew she would take me to the dentist next morning! I could not get what I wanted out of her without getting something more, which I did not want. I wanted immediate relief from pain: but I could not get it without having my teeth set permanently right. And I knew those dentists! I knew they started fiddling about with all sorts of other teeth which had not begun to ache. They would not let sleeping dogs lie; If you gave them an inch they took an ell' (p 167 f).

All over the world Christ is seen as an immensely attractive Person. I find that people are hungry to learn about Him, because God has given to everyone a big spiritual appetite, and that appetite will never be satisfied until we have tasted Christ Himself. The trouble is that Christ will challenge us about any points in our lives which are not right, for if we want to find Christ, we must give those things up, and allow God to have control. This is always the rub. You may know that there are some things in your life which are causing you trouble, like a bad tooth. Yes, you would like Christ to deal with those things immediately. However, what if He starts touching other parts of your life, which you don't want Him to deal with at all? I can simply promise you that He knows what He is doing. He wants you to have the best possible life, and because He loves you, He will not let you go with less than the best.

Who comes first?

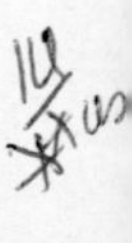

Kierkegaard once shrewdly put it like this: 'It is so hard to believe because it is so hard to obey.' Most of us have a touch of King Herod about us. Herod was a double-minded man: one half of him liked to hear the truth about God, but the other half did not like the moral implications of that truth. So when John the Baptist was in the maximum security wing

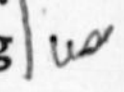

of the palace, every now and then he would be brought out of the dungeon to preach in the Royal Chapel. Herod liked to listen to the Word of God. Unfortunately, however, Herod was guilty of a wrong sexual relationship, and every time John the Baptist was bold enough and rash enough to touch on this point in his sermon (and he did this pretty often) back he went to the maximum security wing! No bread or water for three days! 'It is so hard to believe because it is so hard to obey.'

Christ once described in a parable our natural reaction to His authority: 'We do not want this man to reign over us' (Luke 19.14). Isn't that true? Isn't that our immediate reaction? Perhaps you feel that this is a little unfair. 'I don't think I am quite the rebel that you may imagine,' you may say to me. 'I really do want to go with Christ; I really do want to follow His standards and principles in life. I largely agree with the Sermon on the Mount, and so on.' Do you?

Here is a simple test. Where His standards and your desires point in the same direction, there is no problem. But where they clash, who wins? 'Good Teacher,' said this fine young man whom Jesus loved, 'what must I do to inherit eternal life?' I want to go your way. And Christ, in effect, said, 'No, you don't; because when my will points in one direction, and your will points in the other direction, you still want to have your own way.' 'You lack one thing; go, sell what you have, and give to the poor, and you will have treasure in heaven; and come, follow me' (Mark 10.21). There are many who, coming face to face with the challenge of Christ, find themselves saying, 'Of course I want to go with You, but, Lord, I did not realize that this would involve my friendships, my girl friend or boy friend, my ambition and career, my marriage, my time and money. No, Lord, not that!' However, Christ never lowers the standard of discipleship.

In Luke 14 we find Him making some extraordinarily chilling remarks:

'*If any one comes to me and does not hate his own father and mother and wife and children and brothers and sisters, yes, and even his own life, he cannot be my disciple*' (v. 26). This is simply an idiomatic way of saying that our love for Jesus must be so great that love for our nearest and dearest must be as hatred in comparison. Of course, it does not mean that we must give up all our friends. But if there should be a clash of loyalty, Christ unquestionably must come first. If we are not willing for this we cannot be His disciples.

Whoever does not bear his own cross and come after me, cannot be my disciple (v. 27). This means that we must be willing to go all the way with Christ, whatever it may cost, even martyrdom if need be. Certainly I must be willing for a life of purpose when I lay aside purely selfish pursuits. If we become Christians, Christ has a particular job for each of us to do. Not everyone is called to be a parson or a missionary; we may be called to be Christians in the very jobs that we have so far planned. But wherever we are, and whatever we are doing, we are called to be witnesses to Christ, ready to tell others about Him.

Whoever of you does not renounce all that he has cannot be my disciple (v. 35). This means a policy of 'Christ first' over all that we own. In other words, we must hold everything on an open palm–future, ambitions, possessions, marriage, everything. With everything on an open palm, Christ can take away whatever He wants at any time, and, for that matter, give whatever He wants. What the young man of the story was doing was to close his hand over what he most valued; and Christ said in effect, 'Unless you are willing to open your hand and let your possessions go, you cannot be my disciple' (Luke 14.26–7, 33).

Nevertheless, it is most important to realize that although Christ may demand a great deal (I won't deny that), we simply cannot lose. As someone put it, 'He is no fool who gives what he cannot keep, to gain what he cannot lose'.[1] Or, as Christ expressed it: 'Whoever would save his life will lose it; and whoever loses his life for my sake and the gospel's will save it' (Mark 8.35). If you commit yourself to Christ, and put the whole of your life on an open palm, you cannot lose. Yes, He may take something away (which you could not have kept anyway); but in return He will give you many, many things that you cannot lose–especially the gift of Himself. He will give you life, and all the riches which go with this. 'Truly,' said Jesus, 'there is no man who has left

[1] Jim Elliot, cited in E. Elliot: *Shadow of the Almighty* (Hodder and Stoughton, 1959)

house or wife or brothers or parents or children, for the sake of the kingdom of God, who will not receive manifold more in this time, and in the age to come eternal life' (Luke 18.29–30). He will help you in your friendships; He will guide you in your career and marriage, provided that you let Him have control. What is the alternative? 'What does it profit a man, to gain the whole world and forfeit his life?' (Mark 8.36).

Life at its best

Some people act as though, if they accept God at all, it can only be on their terms. 'He must prove to me this! He must help me with that! He must not interfere with the other!' We are not God's bosses! We are His servants! He is our God! The astonishing fact is that we can in fact come to Him and that we can in fact have His guidance and help. But it must be on His terms. He is God. And again, the amazing thing is this: He is not just lording it over us. In His love He wants the very best for our lives. That is why Christ makes such demands on us as Christians. He offers us all the help, strength, and guidance that we need, but if we are not willing to let Christ have control, He cannot come and do what He wants with us. We must mean business with Him.

Maybe I am optimistic, but I believe that a great many people today are wanting, deep down, to know the purpose in life that God has for them. But if we are not willing for that, we have rejected eternal life and consequently chosen eternal death. The choice is ours.

Tragically, it seems that the young man we have been considering never stopped to consider this alternative to following Jesus. We are told two things about him.

First, *he was sad*. Mark says, 'His countenance fell', which means Christ had challenged him about the one part of his life which he prized above everything: his treasures and possessions. He was profoundly shocked by what Christ had said.

Secondly, *he went away*. Christ never stopped him; He never ran after him; He never said, 'Let's go fifty-fifty'. It is always all or nothing with Christ. And with infinite sadness, no doubt, Christ let go probably the most outstanding young man that He ever met on this earth. He loved him very much indeed, but love risks being rejected, and on this occasion it was.

CHAPTER SEVEN

Conversion—Escape from Reality?

D. H. Lawrence once wrote that no inspiration whatever will get 'weak, impotent, vicious, worthless and rebellious man' beyond his own limits, and therefore Christ's Christianity was doomed to failure. In some ways this was a shrewd and penetrating remark, because D. H. Lawrence was being realistic about man's nature and man's natural inability to fulfil any reasonably demanding code of ethics or philosophy of life. He was not implying that all men are wholly bad and could never do anything good. That is plain nonsense. But he was saying, in effect, that it is no good throwing the Bible, or the Sermon on the Mount, or the Ten Commandments at a person, and saying 'Keep that!' It is quite impossible. Most of us recognize that we cannot live up even to our own standards. And if Christ came merely to underline the Ten Commandments, and intensify their application by referring them to thoughts as well as deeds (which He did), there would be no good news of Christ at all—only a hopeless, legalistic, idealistic, but utterly unrealistic, standard of life, to which no one could ever attain.

This inability of man to live up to a standard set for him pinpoints one of the main differences between Christianity and the other great religions of the world. All other religions say: do this, do that; don't do this, don't do that. They point to a Mount Everest of achievement and say 'That is what you must try to scale by your own determination and discipline'. Christianity, on the other hand, fully recognizes, as did D. H. Lawrence, that man, left to himself, is 'weak, impotent, vicious, worthless and rebellious', unable to keep the Ten Commandments, His Maker's instructions. Therefore it provides him not only with the Saviour to deal with the guilt of the past, but a powerful living Spirit to deal with the present and the future. In some famous words of William Temple:

'It is no good giving me a play like Hamlet or King Lear, and telling me to write a play like that. Shakespeare could do it; I can't. And it is no good showing me a life like the life of Jesus and telling me to live a life like that. Jesus could do it; I can't. But if the genius of Shakespeare could come and live in me, then I could write plays like that. And if the Spirit of Jesus could come and live in me, I could live a life like that.'[1]

That is what Christ had to make clear to Nicodemus, a gifted intellectual who came one night to ask various questions that were on his mind (John 3.1–21). Nicodemus had heard a lot about this astonishing carpenter from Nazareth: how He spoke with authority, healed the sick, cast out demons, and even raised the dead. Why, Jesus was the talking point of the whole city. Here surely was a man who would at last answer the really vital questions on his mind.

Before many minutes, Nicodemus found himself face to face with Jesus. 'Rabbi,' he said with respect (he had his opening speech prepared), 'we know that you are a teacher come from God; for no one can do these signs that you do, unless God is with him.' But Jesus cut him short. The next three words in the story are 'Jesus answered him': strange words, because Nicodemus had so far not asked a single question! But 'Jesus answered him'.

Born Again

Jesus knows the heart and mind of every single person. He knows the secret thoughts, the hidden desires, the innermost problems. And on this occasion, Jesus was saying, in effect, 'Nicodemus, I know that you have one burning question in your mind; that is why you have come to Me. I know there are lots of questions and problems, but above all there is one basic problem: how can God become real to you?' And the answer Jesus gave to Nicodemus was, 'You must be born again'. 'How?' Behind Nicodemus' question lay another, 'Why?' He was a religious man, respectable and upright, a teacher of the Jews, well known in the neighbourhood, and here was this comparatively young man saying to him, of all people, 'You haven't started; you need a new life altogether'. Why?

Jesus gave two clear reasons. First, unless we are born again, we *cannot see the Kingdom of God*. A man once stood on

[1] Quoted in *Basic Christianity*, p 104 f

a soap-box at Hyde Park Corner, pouring scorn on Christianity. 'People tell me that God exists; but I can't see Him. People tell me that there is a life after death; but I can't see it. People tell me that there is a judgment to come; but I can't see it. People tell me that there is a heaven and a hell; but I can't see them...' He won cheap applause, and climbed down from his 'pulpit'. Another struggled on to the soap-box. 'People tell me that there is green grass all round; but I can't see it. People tell me that there is blue sky above; but I can't see it. People tell me that there are trees nearby; but I can't see them. You see, I'm blind!'

Christ made it perfectly clear that unless a man is born again he is spiritually blind. He cannot see the Kingdom of God. Nicodemus could not see. He kept asking, How? 'How can this be?' But Nicodemus was not alone in his blindness. He was suffering from a complaint that many have today. The fact is that when it comes to the greatest and most important facts in the world–the existence of God, the way to heaven, the path of happiness now–man is spiritually blind. He is groping in the dark; he does not know where he is going.

A student who was training to be a teacher once came to me and said, 'I have just realized that I am going to influence hundreds of young people in the future. I shall be guiding them one way or another. The trouble is, I do not know which way I am going myself.' He was right to be concerned, because Christ made it clear that ultimately every person can travel in only one of two directions: the narrow path leading to life, or the broad road leading to destruction.

A business man with money, a secure future, a lovely home, an attractive wife and three children, asked me a few years ago, 'What is the whole purpose of life? I have everything at my feet, and yet I do not know the meaning of life.' He was, in fact, beginning to discover that there is no lasting purpose apart from Christ. He was echoing the words of "Nowhere Man," the Lennon and McCartney song that tells of a nowhere man in a nowhere land making nowhere plans and lacking a point of view and not knowing where he is headed.

A little time ago I received this letter from a young mother:

> 'I will never forget January 13th, 1967, when you helped me to make my big decision (to accept Christ as my Saviour and Lord). During those two weeks you made me understand where I was going . . . I was simply going through life like a blind person who didn't even want to see.'

This was an honest remark because it reveals one of the commonest causes of spiritual blindness; there are none so blind as those who won't see! However, she went on to say, 'Now it is wonderful to have a Friend so near to me all the time, who watches over me, and listens to me wherever I go.' She had found in life the glorious meaning that Christ can bring.

Malcolm Muggeridge, preaching at Edinburgh in January 1968, said,

> 'I come back . . . to the Christian notion that man's efforts to make himself permanently happy are doomed to failure. He must indeed, as Christ said, be born again . . . As far as I am concerned, it is Christ or nothing.'

Man's spiritual blindness becomes obvious if one listens to a religious conversation amongst those who are not committed Christians; often they refer to God as some vague thing, a subject for debate and argument. We are by nature utterly blind to the fact of God's holiness and majesty; not seeing that in His hand is our very breath and life. Others again stand Christ, as it were, as a prisoner in the dock, while *they pass their judgment on Him!* Once again, they are blind to the fact that by their verdicts they themselves are being judged.

I remember talking to an intelligent student studying criminology. We talked and talked about the Christian faith, and he just could not see it and could not understand what it was all about. However, the time came when, humbly and simply, he asked Christ into his life. At once he saw it! I used to read the Bible with him, and about a month after he had taken this step of faith he said to me, 'Now I see it all. I feel like a little child starting again from scratch.' He was born again. But if this inner rebirth does not take place a man cannot *see* the kingdom of God. That is the first statement that Jesus made to Nicodemus.

Secondly, unless we are born again, we *cannot enter the kingdom of God*. If we choose to be independent of God, to go our own way, persistently to break the greatest commandment there is (loving God with all our heart, mind, soul and strength), then why on earth do we imagine that we can sail into God's presence when the moment comes? The truth is, of course, that we cannot. Christ had to go to the cross and die in our place and bear our sin before we could possibly come into God's presence. He had to remove the one great barrier which separates man from God, the barrier of sin. Christ died to bring us to God. There is no other way. Apart from the cross of Christ, there is no hope whatsoever. Therefore, if a person has chosen to live his life separated from God, then separated from God he will be! It is his own choice.

Bishop Taylor Smith, former Chaplain-General of the British Forces, was once preaching in a large cathedral. In order to emphasize the necessity of this new birth, he said:

> 'My dear people, do not substitute anything for the new birth. You may be a member of a church, but church membership is not new birth, and "except a man be born again, he cannot see the kingdom of God." '

On his left sat the Archdeacon in his stall. Pointing directly at him, he said:

> 'You might even be an archdeacon like my friend in his stall and not be born again, and "except a man be born again, he cannot see the kingdom of God". You might even be a bishop like myself, and not be born again, and "except a man be born again, he cannot see the kingdom of God".'

A day or so later he received a letter from the Archdeacon, in which he wrote:

> 'My dear Bishop: You have found me out. I have been a clergyman for over thirty years, but I have never known anything of the joy that Christians speak of. I never could understand it. Mine has been a hard, legal service. I did not know what the matter was with me, but when you pointed

directly at me, and said, "You might even be an archdeacon and not be born again", I realised in a moment what the trouble was. I had never known anything of the new birth.'

The next day the Bishop and the Archdeacon met and looked at the Bible together; and after some hours, both were on their knees, the Archdeacon taking his place before God as a sinner, and telling Christ that he would trust Him as his Saviour. From that moment everything was different. It does not matter who you are: theologian, ordinand, lecturer, minister, bishop; 'you must be born again'. Those are the words of Christ, the Son of God.

A Few Objections

Many people have told me that they make objections as convenient excuses for trying to keep Christ at arm's length, so that they do not have to get involved. To say so is honest. Perhaps the key question is, 'If someone answered all your objections would you accept Christ as your Saviour and Lord?' If the answer is 'No' there is no point in going on. However, clearly there is such a thing as a genuine, honest seeker, and therefore it is right to look briefly at some of the most common difficulties.

'*I find all this too emotional.*' Whenever someone levels the charge of emotionalism I am interested to see the person who makes that remark. What is he like? Is he a dessicated intellectual? Has he no emotions at all? Christ is concerned with the whole man: body, mind, heart, and will. To by-pass the mind altogether and whip up the emotions is something I am as much against as anyone else. But true Christianity does not leave the emotions untouched. The only thing which has no emotions is a dead body, and if your faith is without emotion it is a dead faith.

Supposing that someone said, 'I'm frightened of marriage: it is all to emotional!' Well, of course, it involves the emotions! It is the commitment of one's total life to another. It is a terrible marriage if no emotions are involved. Do not be frightened of your emotions when you give your life to Christ; though for many people, this is a comparatively unemotional experience.

'*I have tried before to be a Christian, but it hasn't worked.*'

I have sympathy if that is your position; you may naturally be hesitant about another step of faith. But it is worth asking two questions. First, did you ever before really ask Christ to come into your life, or did you simply start doing 'Christian' things? You can quite easily turn over a new leaf without beginning a new life. Secondly, if you really did ask Christ to come in, have you gone on with that friendship? Every true friendship needs to be developed and deepened. As soon as you take it for granted, it will fade altogether.

However, if you feel that you have tried before and that it hasn't worked, I would say: 'Don't analyse too carefully what happened or what did not happen in the past. You may have done it, as it were, in pencil already. Now, ink it over. Make it definite.' I have known many people who have come through to a clear personal relationship with Christ by doing just that.

'Isn't it presumptuous to be definite and to say that "my" God is real?' 'Isn't it more humble to say that I am seeking for Him, trying my best, without being too definite about it?' Of course not! Your eternal future depends on your relationship with God. Of course God wants you to know, beyond any shadow of doubt. The first letter of John was written for this very purpose: 'I write this to you who believe in the name of the Son of God, that you may know that you have eternal life' (1 John 5.13). Throughout the letter John gives very carefully the tests by which a person may know whether or not he has eternal life.

Suppose that you asked me, 'Are you married?' What would you think if I replied, 'Well, I think so. I am doing my best. I wash up the breakfast things, get the coal in, give her the housekeeping money and buy her clothes. Yes' (with a sigh), 'I think I must be married!' That is ridiculous! If you asked me, 'Are you married?' my answer would be 'Yes, because on 19th September 1964, I committed my life, for better for worse, for richer for poorer, to Elizabeth Anne McEwan-Smith; and I have never been the same since!' That is how I know I am married. It is almost exactly the same with being born again. I know I am born again, because on 6th October 1954, I committed my life for better (not for worse), for richer (not for poorer), to Jesus Christ, my Saviour and Lord. I have never been the same since! That is how I know

I am born again. It is not presumptuous. God longs for each one of us to know, and to be able to say, 'My God is real'.

'I could never keep it up.' 'I know I would be exactly the same in a few weeks' time.' There are two things to say about this. First, you will never be quite the same if you truly accept Christ into your life. You will be born again, and a member of God's family. You will have a new relationship with God altogether, which is now fixed. John says in his Gospel, 'To all who received him, who believed in his name, he gave power to become children of God' (John 1.12). Secondly, you are not asked to keep up this Christian life in your own strength. The glorious news for the Christian is that Christ is able to keep him from falling. Jesus said, 'I give them eternal life, and they shall never perish, and no one shall snatch them out of my hand' (John 10.28). When you become a Christian, the Spirit of God comes to dwell in your whole being. The same power that raised Jesus from the dead is now in your life. The same power that took away the fear from those first disciples and sent them out with boldness and courage is now with you. You may be afraid of your showing as a Christian in front of your friends. You will never have to stand on your own: the Spirit of God will guide you and help you, if only you let Him.

It is not a continuous struggle all the time, for the Christian. The more you rest in Christ's strength, Christ's faithfulness, Christ's love, and Christ's peace, the more He will live out His life in you. He wants to help you all the way, in all your decisions, in matters of guidance, in problems and in difficulties. He comes, as He once said, to give you rest.

The reality of the effects of the Spirit's presence can clearly be seen in the New Testament, and especially in the Acts of the Apostles. When the gift of the Spirit came down upon those first Christians, the whole scene was utterly transformed. The story of the birth and growth of the Christian Church from a tiny band of frightened men and women is quite remarkable. In the words of J. B. Phillips, 'Even if I were not myself a convinced Christian, I should find it impossible to explain this strange phenomenon'.[1]

A university student asked me, a little while ago, 'If all the

[1] J. B. Phillips: *Ring of Truth* (Hodder and Stoughton, 1967), p 28

Bibles in the world were destroyed tomorrow' (I love these hypothetical questions!) 'what evidence would there be for the Christian faith? Is God at work today? Are people born again today? How can I know that Christ is alive? How can we know that God is real?' I could write many books in answer to that. If I did not see the Spirit of God manifestly at work in the lives of individuals week in, week out, I should certainly find it hard to go on preaching the Christian faith with any assurance.

When a person commits himself to Christ and is born again by the Spirit of God, exciting things begin to happen. This is no vague theory. The new birth concerns *life*. This is how Paul put it: 'If any one is in Christ, he is a new creation' (2 Corinthians 5.17). In the Greek it is even more forceful than that. There is no verb in the second part of the sentence, so that it really reads like a startling headline: If any one is in Christ—new creation! Paul goes on, 'the old has passed away, behold, the new has come'. Concerning human nature, Jesus once said, 'Make the tree good, and its fruit good' (Matthew 12.33). Of course! That is obvious! But the problem which has defied man down the ages is, how do you make the tree good? How do you change the human heart? How can you make selfish man unselfish? How can you make a person control his tongue? This is an important question. The Bible rightly says that 'no human being can tame the tongue' (James 3.8). A gipsy once wrote:

> 'No scientist is as sure of the working of any law, no physician is as sure of any medicine, no mathematician is as sure of any axiom, as I am that Jesus Christ came into my gipsy tent and converted my rough, swearing, drinking, pilfering, gipsy father into a clean, tender, honourable, strong, beautiful Christian man.'

Temple Gairdner made his personal comment on the words 'behold all things are become new' (2 Corinthians 5.17 AV):

> 'This sense of newness is simply delicious. It makes new the Bible, and friends, and all mankind, and love, and spiritual things, and Sunday, and church, and God Himself.'[1]

Richard Wurmbrand, having suffered greatly at the hands

[1] Quoted by H. A. Evan Hopkins in *Henceforth* (I.U.P. 1942) p 5

of communists, speaks of the reality of Christ in a filthy prison cell:

> 'I have seen Christians in communist prisons with fifty pounds of chains on their feet, tortured with red hot iron pokers, in whose throats spoonfuls of salt have been forced being kept afterwards without water, starving, whipped, suffering from cold and praying with fervour for the communists. This is humanly inexplicable! It is the love of Christ which was shed into our hearts...[1]

Every week I talk with people, or receive letters from people, who have discovered what it is to be a new creation in Christ, and to know the Spirit of Christ transforming their lives.

There is one further important comment that I must make in this chapter. When Christ says, 'You must be born again', it is not just pious advice. It is not just His own personal opinion. It is a *command!* Christ is the Son of God and the King of kings. He does not say something without meaning it and without urgency and authority. In John 3 there is an interesting, though solemn, progression of statements about Jesus Christ:

> 'Whoever believes in Him may have eternal life' (verse 15).
>
> 'Whoever believes in Him shall not perish' (verse 16).
>
> 'He who does not believe is condemned already' (verse 18).
>
> 'He who does not obey the Son shall not see life, but the wrath of God rests upon him' (verse 36).

Step by step we are warned with increasing solemnity and severity. Therefore, says Jesus, 'You must be born again'. Christ knows that one day He must judge the world, and then He will have to underline the decision that each of us has made about Him. If you say now, and in the future, 'Depart from me—I do not want you as my Saviour and Lord', then one day He must act on that decision. He will say to you, 'Depart from Me!'

But Christ did not come into the world to condemn, but to save. And because He loves us, He says with great urgency and feeling, 'You must be born again'.

[1] *Tortured for Christ* (Hodder and Stoughton, 1967), p 52

CHAPTER EIGHT

Commitment

The question is, How? It is all very well being told 'You must be born again', 'You must come to Christ', 'You must find the Reality of God in your experience'. The question is, how? Jesus once said, 'Seek, and you will find'; but there are many who complain that they have sought–at some time or other–but have never found. Here in this final chapter I want to explain, as simply as I can, what it means to find Christ and how it is possible to say 'My God is Real'.

Finding the Reality of God

Wherever the first disciples went, they preached one message which could be summarized in two words: *Repent* and *Believe*. What do these words mean?

Repent. This means 'About Turn', or, more accurately, a change of mind leading to a change of direction. If in any journey you realize that you have been going in the wrong direction, as soon as you turn round and start going in the right direction you begin to make progress.

Therefore, before any person can find Christ, he must humbly admit that he has been going in the wrong direction: 'I've been going *my* own way, doing what *I* want, not what God wants.' If we look at God's laws, or at the teaching and example of Christ Himself, it is quite clear that on countless occasions we have not followed His instructions but gone our own way instead–a way, said Christ, which leads us finally to destruction–an eternal separation from God and from everything good.

In practical terms, repentance involves two decisions. First, you must be willing, with the help of Christ, to let go anything which you know is wrong. It may be big or small. But if on any point God touches your conscience or shows you in His Word that something is not right in His eyes, you must be willing to give up. You may not be able to do so in your own strength. Habits die hard. But if you are willing to let it go, then Christ will help to put that thing right.

Secondly, you must be willing to go with Christ in the future, wherever He may lead you. 'If any man would come after me, let him deny himself and take up his cross and follow me.'[1] I have written more fully about this in Chapter six (pp 68–77). But basically it means Christ First—first in your friendships and relationships, first in your job and in your home, first with your money and possessions, first in your love and marriage, first in your ambitions and in your future. The whole of your life must be on an 'open palm', so that Christ can take away what He wants when He wants, and He can give you what He wants when He wants. Let me at once say that He comes to enrich your life at every point; if He takes something away it is only because He has something better in store for you.

> 'For whoever would save his life will lose it; and whoever loses his life for my sake and the gospel's will save it. For what does it profit a man, to gain the whole world and forfeit his life'.[2]

He must also be unashamed of Christ in front of others: not always 'preaching' at them, but openly and unashamedly a true committed Christian.

Believe. There are various truths that a Christian must believe: above all that through Christ's death and resurrection it is possible for us to have a personal relationship with the Living God (see Chapters four and five).

But 'belief' in the New Testament involves action. If I believe in Christ I commit myself unreservedly to Him. Any 'belief' short of this is not true Christian belief. James asks in his letter, with a touch of scorn, 'So you believe that there is one God? That's fine. So do all the devils in hell, and shudder in terror!'[3]

One way of illustrating Christian belief is by the Anglican Marriage Service! When I was married, the minister asked me, 'David, will you have this woman?' I said 'I will'. Turning to my wife he said 'Anne, will you have this man?' She said 'I will'. The moment we *both* said 'I will', *that*

[1] Mark 8.34 [2] Mark 8.35
[3] James 2.19 (J. B. Phillips)

moment a new relationship was fixed and established. Let me now dramatize Christian commitment like this:

'Saviour, will you have this sinner?' Always, on every occasion, no matter who the sinner may be or what sins he has committed, Jesus replies 'I will'. The vital question is now, therefore:

'Sinner, will you have this Saviour?' As soon as you say 'I will', and really mean it, a new relationship will be fixed and established. Through Christ you will be able to say, with increasing conviction and joy, 'My God is Real'.

This analogy is perhaps useful for two further reasons. First, at my wedding when I said 'I will', I don't think I had any feelings at all; if anything I felt numb! Similarly when you say 'I will' to Jesus you may feel nothing and be tempted to wonder whether there is any reality at all. Let me stress that feelings are comparatively unimportant at this stage and at every stage of our Christian life. The important point in commitment is an act of *will*, and Christ promises: 'Him who comes to me I *will not*' (double negative in the Greek—very strong) 'cast out.' Trust His Word and believe that you now have a permanent relationship with Him.

Secondly, when I said 'I will' at my wedding, this was only the beginning of a new life. Much more was to follow. To be honest, the first year was somewhat rough at times. The new relationship had to be worked out, and many adjustments had to be made. So it is with Christ. This step is only a beginning, but it is a vital beginning.

If you have never taken this step before, or if you are not sure about it, then let me encourage you to 'launch out' if you are ready. As I said earlier, you may have done it in pencil before. Well, there is no harm in inking it over, so that from now on you can be absolutely sure that you have given your life personally to Jesus Christ and that you belong to Him for ever. If you are not ready, then don't take this step. But there is an urgency whenever we understand the heart of the Christian message: 'Seek the Lord while he may be found, call upon him while he is near.'[1] He is not always to be found; He is not always near. We can't pick and choose our moment to come to Him.

[1] Isaiah 55.6

If, therefore, you have never taken this step, or are not sure and would like to be sure, here is a prayer which you could make your own:

'Lord Jesus Christ, I admit that I have sinned and gone my own way. I am willing to turn from what I know is wrong, and I am willing to follow You and to go wherever you lead. Thank you for dying on the Cross to bear away my sin. And now I come to You, Lord Jesus. I say "I will". I ask you to be my Saviour and Friend and Lord for ever. Thank you Lord Jesus. Amen.'

Proving the Reality of God

If you have just prayed that prayer then this is the beginning of a new and wonderful friendship with the Lord Jesus which can and must be deepened over the months and years. Let us look at Saul of Tarsus to see what happened to him when he met with the Risen Christ on the road to Damascus and what were some of the immediate consequences of this vital encounter. There are a number of points from Acts 9 which will help you to prove the reality of God in your own personal experience.

He trusted Christ's Word.

> 'Now as he journeyed he approached Damascus, and suddenly a light from heaven flashed about him. And he fell to the ground and heard a voice saying to him, "Saul, Saul, why do you persecute me?" And he said, "Who are you, Lord?" And he said, "I am Jesus, whom you are persecuting.."' (v. 3–5).

It is quite clear from what follows that he trusted this word of Christ. In one sense it is very remarkable. Until that moment he had been fiercely opposed to Christ and to the disciples; and suddenly he is challenged by the Risen Saviour. It is not a very intellectual challenge; and there must have been endless questions which were still unanswered in his mind. But the voice said 'I am Jesus', and he trusted Christ's word.

Faith means taking God at His word. It is so important to grasp this, so that your Christian life does not go up and down depending on feelings and experiences. It is Christ's faithfulness that ultimately counts. He really means what He says. Paul later gave Abraham as the supreme example of faith, and in Romans 4 he writes about Abraham: 'No distrust made him waver concerning the promise of God, but he grew strong in his faith as he gave glory to God, fully convinced that God was able to do what he had promised.' This is the essence of faith. Of course, a real faith in Christ will result in a transformation of your life. John, in his first letter, explains that some of the marks of the new life which Christ brings are a new joy, a new desire to please God, a new hatred of sin, a new love for Christians, a new peace in your heart, a new strength to overcome temptation, and a new reality in prayer. These will not all appear overnight, but there should be increasing evidence in your life of the reality of Christ's promise. Don't be worried if you have occasional doubts. Every Christian has at some time or other, especially a few weeks after a decisive step of personal commitment to Christ. However, we can counter these doubts by claiming and trusting a promise of Christ.

He began to pray. God told Ananias to go to Saul of Tarsus, 'for behold, he is praying' (v. 11). This was the first thing that Saul did after his meeting with Christ on that road. Of course, Saul had been a very religious man and prayer was nothing new to him. But now for the first time he was talking intimately to a God who had become real.

This pin-points one of the main essentials in a continuing relationship with Christ. All friendships and relationships must be developed or else they are in danger of fading away. Perhaps the greatest secret of all in the Christian life is to spend some time with Christ every day. Christ Himself gave us the pattern to follow. In Mark 1.35 we read something about a day in the life of the Master: 'And in the morning, a great while before day, he rose and went out to a lonely place, and there he prayed.' Notice that the time was 'in the morning, a great while before day'! This, for the majority of people, is by far the most satisfactory time to be alone with God. Someone has said that the two main essentials for the Christian life are a Bible and an alarm clock. Certainly there is need for firm discipline on this point, as you will never find it easy. But if you develop the habit of getting up that much earlier to spend time alone with Christ every day, you will be tremendously grateful for this habit as the time goes on. Notice also the place where Christ prayed: it was 'a lonely place'. It is essential that you find somewhere that you can be alone and undisturbed for an unhurried time for Bible reading and prayer. Some system of Bible study will be invaluable, and many people have found Scripture Union Notes to be a good guide for such regular study.

It will also be a help if you can read the Bible and study it with a Christian friend. You may well find certain questions arising in your mind or certain problems which seem difficult to solve, and developing a friendship with another Christian so that you can share these questions and problems together will prove of immense value to you. Start reading good Christian books also; there are many of these on the market, and no doubt a Christian friend will give you some guidance on this point.

He was willing to be known. Immediately he was baptized (v. 18), and by this, apart from other meanings of baptism, he was openly confessing his faith in Jesus Christ. For Saul of Tarsus this was a tremendous step; he really burnt his boats, and it certainly was not easy for him. However, in my experience, the Christians who have gone on with Christ have always been those who unashamedly have confessed their faith in Christ to their unbelieving friends. The secret disciple has a terrible struggle. But if you confess Christ openly to other people, as the opportunity arises, you will find that the reality of His presence will steadily increase.

He made friends with other Christians. It is worth seeing in this passage that this wasn't so easy for Saul: 'And when he had come to Jerusalem he attempted to join the disciples; and they were all afraid of him, for they did not believe that he was a disciple' (v. 26). However, he persisted and soon he was thoroughly involved with other Christians. The New Testament knows nothing of the isolated Christian. Every person who committed his life to Christ automatically joined in with other Christians. They came from various backgrounds, had different personalities, and some of them found that their temperaments clashed. Nevertheless, to remain apart from Christian fellowship would have been to court disaster. Every Christian needs a live fellowship of true believers who know and love the Lord Jesus, who are studying His word, and seeking to serve Him in the community. If you do not know of such a fellowship in your immediate area, do your utmost to seek one out. There will almost certainly be a group of such disciples somewhere, and you will find it of immense personal help if you throw in your lot with them.

He tried to tell others. 'And in the synagogues immediately he proclaimed Jesus, saying, "He is the Son of God"' (v. 30). It is worth noticing that he went straight to the place where he was known. Certainly your prime responsibility for Christian witness will be amongst your friends and your circle of acquaintances. If you think of it, you have a unique responsibility here, because no one else in the whole world has the same circle of friends and acquaintances. What can you say to them? Well, once again, don't preach at them, but when the opportunity arises give a personal testimony of how you found Christ, and what He has come to mean to you. Also, as soon as possible, learn the basic steps towards a personal relationship with Christ, and learn a number of simple verses to guide a friend to the same relationship that you have found yourself. In the first half of this chapter I gave one way of explaining the steps to Christ; here is another way which I have found to be of great value over the years.

(a) *Admit your need*

The fact of sin–Romans 3.23; 1 John 3.4; Matthew 22.37.

The consequences of sin–Rom. 6.23; 1 John 1.5–6; Isaiah 59.1–2.

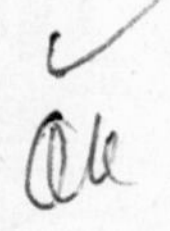

(b) *Believe that Christ died for you.*

Isaiah 53.5–6; 1 Peter 2.24; 3.18.

(c) *Count the Cost*

1. Repentance–Isaiah 55.7
2. Surrender –Mark 8.34
3. Witness –Romans 10.9–10

} or Mark 8.34–38.

(d) *Come to Him*

John 1.12 and Revelation 3.20 } or { Matthew 11.28 and John 6.37.

His life showed a difference. 'And all who heard him were amazed, and said, "Is not this the man who made havoc in Jerusalem...?"' (v. 21). Right from the start Saul impressed those who knew him by the marked difference that Christ had made in his life. This, of course, was one of the outstanding features of Christ Himself: that although He mixed with every kind of person, He was always quite different. This was part of His immense attractiveness. People marvelled at His graciousness and love and compassion. A Christian is not called to obey hundreds of rules. He is called to walk with Jesus. Therefore, concerning any questionable activities or pursuits, the practical test is, can I really pray about this? Can I do this knowing that Christ is with me? The Bible, in fact, gives us three guidelines for all that we say and do:

(*a*) Will it help or hinder my Christian life? (see Hebrews 12.1).
(*b*) Will it help or hinder someone else's Christian life? (see 1 Corinthians 8).
(*c*) Is it to the glory of God? (see 1 Corinthians 10.31).

He was filled with the Holy Spirit. When Ananias came to Saul he laid his hands on him and said, 'Brother Saul, the Lord Jesus who appeared to you on the road by which you came, has sent me that you may regain your sight and be filled with the Holy Spirit.' (v. 17). This was the key to the whole of his life and ministry. Without this he would have been empty, powerless, struggling to do what he felt was right but with no strength to accomplish it. The greatest need for each Christian is to learn what it is to be filled with the Holy Spirit, and to go on being filled with the Holy Spirit day by day. Jesus once made a promise, in Luke chapter 11, to those who were conscious that they had 'nothing to set before' those in need. He said 'If you then, who are evil, know how to give good gifts to your children, how much more will the heavenly Father give the Holy Spirit to those who ask him!' (v. 13). If you long to know the fullness of God's power in your life, humbly claim this promise and pray that your Heavenly Father might fill you with the power of His Spirit that you might be able to witness to Jesus boldly and clearly. The Holy Spirit is the One who makes Jesus more real to you, and who will guide you and teach you from God's word as you study it daily. Let Him possess and control your life day by day, and you will increasingly be able to say, with absolute conviction, *My God is Real.*

A certain man came to his pastor by day, saying "Sir, what shall a church member do who does not believe in the Chr. religion, who is not even sure of God?" "The pastor listened. "Shall he withdraw his membership?" The pastor loved the man — & respected him, now not only because he was a professional man, a physician, but a person of integrity. "Surely, that is not sufficient reason for leaving, for others among us are in the search for God! But as you will." It seemed, altho the pastor may have been mistaken that as this distinguished man spoke — his eyes said, "But I wish God were real to me, so I could believe." & Jews I Messiah will come

Sun serv.